FRETBOARD ROADMAPS

Essential Guitar Patterns
That All the Pros Know & Use

2nd EDITION

BY FRED SOKOLOW

Editorial Assistance by Ronnie Schiff

ISBN-13: 978-0-7935-2088-6

HAL•LEONARD®
CORPORATION
7777 W. BLUEMOUND RD. P.O. BOX 13819 MILWAUKEE, WI 53213

In Australia Contact:
Hal Leonard Australia Pty. Ltd.
4 Lentara Court
Cheltenham, Victoria, 3192 Australia
Email: ausadmin@halleonard.com

Visit Hal Leonard Online at
www.halleonard.com

CONTENTS

INTRODUCTION

There are moveable patterns on the guitar fretboard that help you think like a musician and enable you to play chords, licks, scales, and progressions in all keys. The pros are aware of these fretboard roadmaps, even if they do not read music. Whether you play rock, blues, jazz, country, or classical music, these roadmaps are *essential guitar knowledge*.

You need the fretboard roadmaps if...

- All your lead guitar playing sounds the same and you want some different styles and flavors from which to choose.

- Some keys are harder to play in than others.

- You can't automatically play any melody you can think of or hum.

- You know some tunes sound alike, but you still learn each chord progression as if it were the only one of its kind.

- Your chord vocabulary is limited, and you memorize new chords slowly, without knowing how they're structured.

- You know a lot of "bits and pieces" on the guitar, but you don't have a system that ties them all together.

Read on, and many guitar mysteries will be explained. Having written over a hundred guitar books, I can say this is the only one that is required reading for my guitar students—at least the ones who are serious.

Good luck,

Fred Sokolow

HOW TO READ CHORD GRIDS

A *chord grid* is a picture of several frets of the guitar's fretboard. The dots show you where to fret (finger) the strings.

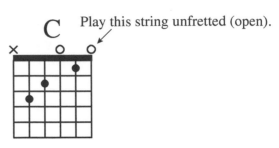

Play this string unfretted (open).

Numbers under a grid indicate the fingering. The number to the right of the grid is a *fret number*.

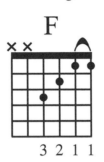

Left Hand

HOW TO READ FRETBOARD DIAGRAMS

Each *fretboard diagram* is a schematic picture of the guitar's fretboard, as it appears when you look down at it while playing.
- The sixth, heaviest string is at the bottom; the first, lightest string is on top.
- Crucial fret numbers such as 5, 7, and 9 are indicated underneath the grid.
- *Dots* on the fretboard indicate where you fret the strings (as in chord grids).
- *Numbers* on the fretboard indicate which finger to use (1 = index finger; 2 = middle finger; etc.).
- *Letters* on the fretboard are notes (A, B♭, C♯, etc.).
- *Roman Numerals* (I, IV, etc.) on the fretboard are roots of chords.

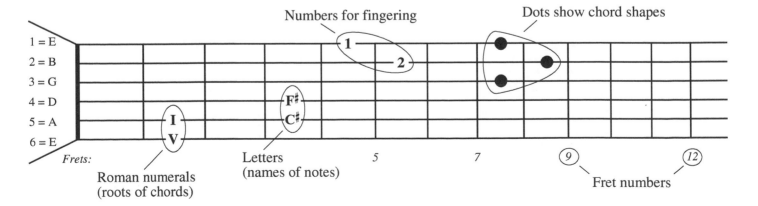

4

HOW TO READ TABLATURE

Songs, scales, and exercises in this book are written in standard music notation and tablature. The six lines of the tablature staff represent the six guitar strings.

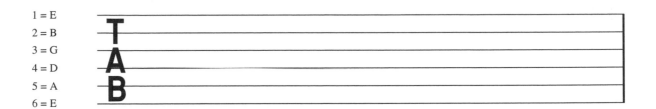

```
1 = E
2 = B
3 = G      T
4 = D      A
5 = A      B
6 = E
```

A number on a line tells you which string to play and where to fret it.

This example means "play the third string on the fourth fret"

This example means "play the fourth string unfretted"

Chords can also be written in tablature: ⟶

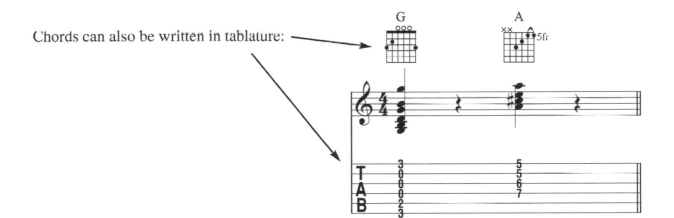

GUITAR NOTATION LEGEND
All the details of tablature notation (hammer-ons, slides, etc.) are explained in the *guitar notation legend* at the back of this book.

NOTES ON THE FRETBOARD

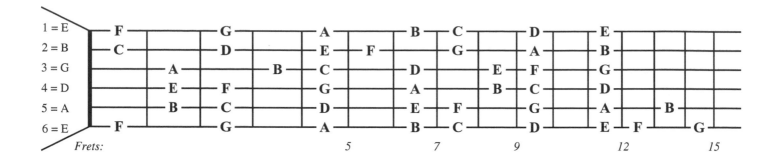

WHY?

Knowing where the notes are will help you find chords and scales up and down the neck. It will also help you construct, alter, and understand chords (e.g., "How do I flat the seventh in this chord? What makes this chord minor instead of major?"). And, if you ever want to read standard music notation (for instance, read a melody in a songbook), you need to know where the notes are.

WHAT?

The notes get higher in pitch as you go up the alphabet and up the fretboard.

A whole step is two frets, and a half step is one fret. Most notes are a whole step apart (C to D is two frets; D to E is two frets), but there are half steps in two places: B to C is one fret, and E to F is one fret.

Sharps are one fret higher: 6th string/3rd fret = G, so 6th string/4th fret = G♯. 6th string/8th fret = C, so 6th string/9th fret = C♯.

Flats are one fret lower: 6th string/5th fret = A, so 6th string/4th fret = A♭. 6th string/10th fret = D, so 6th string/9th fret = D♭.

Some notes have two names: 6th string/4th fret is both G♯ and A♭. The name you use depends on the musical context.

HOW?

Fretboard markings help. Most guitars have fretboard inlays or marks somewhere on the neck indicating the 5th, 7th, 9th, and 12th frets. Be aware of these signposts! Once you have memorized the fact that the 6th string/5th fret = A, the fretboard mark on fret 5 helps you get there fast.

Everything starts over at the 12th fret. The 12th fret is like a second nut. The 6th string three frets above the nut is G; the 6th string three frets above fret 12 is also G.

The 6th and 1st strings are the same. When you memorize the 6th-string notes, you also have the 1st-string notes.

DO IT!   **Start by memorizing the notes on the 6th and 5th strings.** You will need to know these notes very soon, for **ROADMAP #3**.

Walk up the 6th string, naming the notes as you go. Start with the letter-only names (F, G, etc.), then add the sharps and/or flats.

Spot-check yourself on the 6th string. Play random notes, out of order, naming them as you play them.

Learn the 5th-string notes the same way. Walk up the string naming the notes, then spot-check yourself playing random notes.

Play 6th- and 4th-string octaves to learn the 4th-string notes. When you use the hand position shown in the adjacent chord grid to play the 6th and 4th strings simultaneously, the 4th-string note is the same note as the one on the 6th string, only it's an *octave* (eight notes) higher. Once you have memorized the notes on the 6th string, this is a shortcut to learning the 4th-string notes.

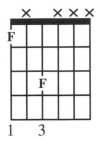

After playing a lot of octaves, walk up the 4th string, naming the notes as you go. Continue using the 6th string as a reference point. Then spot-check yourself on the 4th string the same way you did on the 6th string.

Play 5th- and 3rd-string octaves to learn the 3rd-string notes. You can relate the 3rd string to the 5th-string notes:

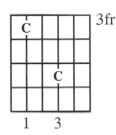

Walk up the 2nd string, naming notes as you go. Then play random notes on the 2nd string and name them as you play them.

SUMMING UP—NOW YOU KNOW...

1. The location of the notes on the fretboard, especially on the 5th and 6th strings

2. The meaning of these musical terms:
    a) Sharp (♯)
    b) Flat (♭)
    c) Whole Step
    d) Half Step

THE MAJOR SCALE

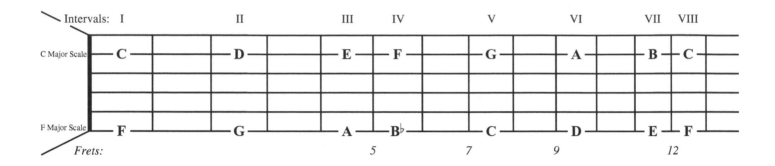

WHY? The major scale is a ruler that helps you measure distances between notes and chords. Knowing the major scale will help you understand and talk about chord construction, scales, and chord relationships.

WHAT? **The major scale is the "Do-Re-Mi" scale you have heard all your life.** Countless familiar tunes are composed of notes from this scale.

Intervals are distances between notes. The intervals of the major scale are used to describe these distances. For example, E is the third note of the C major scale, and it is four frets above C (see above). This distance, or interval, is called a *third*. Similarly, A is a third above F, and C♯ is a 3rd above A. On the guitar, *a third is always a distance of four frets.*

The intervals of a second, third, sixth and seventh can be major or minor. *Major* means "as in the major scale," and *minor* means flatted, or lowered one fret. For instance, E is a major third (four frets) above C, so E♭ is a minor third (three frets) above C.

An octave is the interval of eight notes. It encompasses the scale. From C to the next highest C is an octave. Notes an octave apart sound alike. They are the same note at different pitches. In other words, all Cs sound alike, as do all Ds, all Es, etc.

Music is played in keys. A key gives a piece of music a home base. A song in the key of C uses melody notes from the C major scale and usually ends on a C note and a C chord.

Tension and resolution: When you leave the home base or tonic chord (for example, a C chord, in the key of C) it causes musical *tension*. That tension is *resolved* when you return to the home base, the tonic chord.

HOW? Every major scale has the same interval pattern of whole and half steps.

C Major Scale

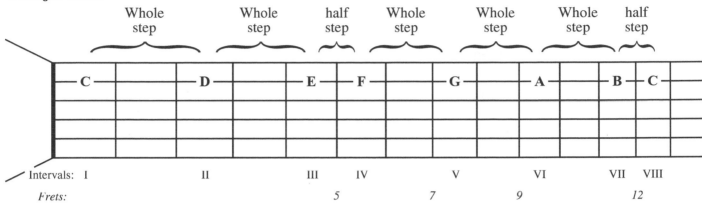

	Whole step		Whole step		half step	Whole step		Whole step		Whole step		half step

	C			D		E	F		G		A		B	C

Intervals: I   II   III   IV   V   VI   VII   VIII

Frets: 5   7   9   12

In other words, the major scale ascends by *whole steps* (two frets at a time) with two exceptions: there is a *half step* (one fret) from the third to the fourth note and from the seventh to the eighth note.

Every interval can be described in terms of frets. A second is two frets, a major third is four frets, an octave is twelve frets, and so on.

Intervals can also be found on the fretboard by relating them to the 6th and 5th strings, like the octaves in the previous chapter:

3rd

4th
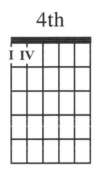

5th
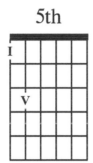

6th
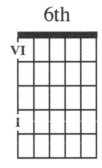

Flatted 7th
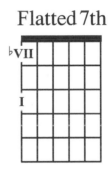

7th
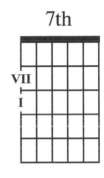

Intervals can extend above the octave. They correspond to lower intervals:

— A *ninth* is two frets above the octave. It is the same note as the *second*, but an octave higher.

— An *eleventh* is five frets above the octave. It is the same note as the *fourth*, but an octave higher.

— A *thirteenth* is nine frets above the octave. It is the same note as the *sixth*, but an octave higher.

C Major Scale

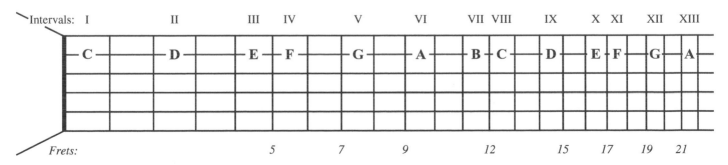

Intervals: I   II   III   IV   V   VI   VII   VIII   IX   X   XI   XII   XIII

	C			D		E	F		G		A		B	C		D		E	F		G	A

Frets: 5   7   9   12   15   17   19   21

Key Signatures: Every major scale (except C) contains some sharps or flats. They are identified in the *key signature* in music notation. A key signature precedes any piece of music and lets the performer know that certain notes are to be played either sharp or flat throughout the piece.

— **Here are the most frequently used key signatures.** Become familiar with all of them.

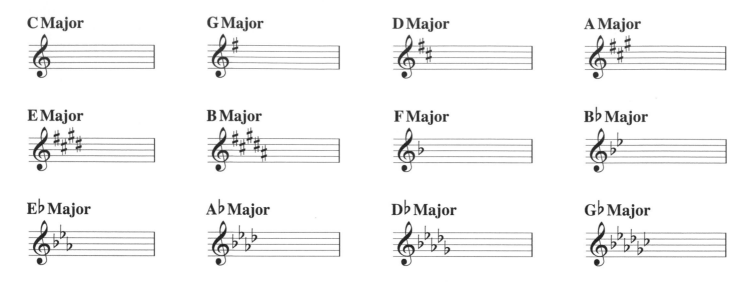

C Major   G Major   D Major   A Major

E Major   B Major   F Major   B♭ Major

E♭ Major   A♭ Major   D♭ Major   G♭ Major

DO IT!   To learn the major scale intervals and key signatures…

— **Play any note and find the note that is a third higher, a fourth and fifth higher, etc.** Do this by counting up the right amount of frets on a single string, and by relating the interval to the 5th or 6th strings.

— **Play major scales on a single string.** Walk up the string, naming the notes as you go:

E Major Scale

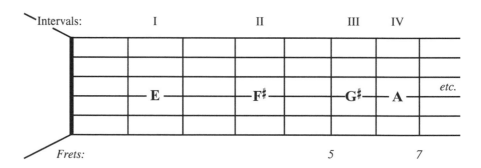

B♭ Major Scale

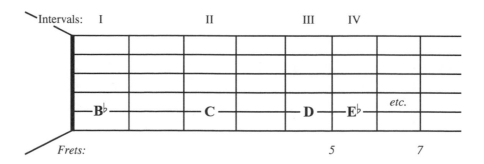

— **Analyze chords for notes and intervals.** A *chord* is three or more notes played simultaneously. Every type of chord (major, minor, etc.) has an *interval formula*. For instance, a major chord is made of 1, 3, and 5. Therefore, a C major chord will consist of the first, third, and fifth notes in the C major scale: C (1), E (3), and G (5).

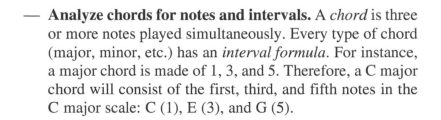

— As shown in these fretboard grids, you can look at any chord and name the notes it contains, and the intervals they represent. The note that gives the chord its name (such as the E in E7) tells you which major scale you are using.

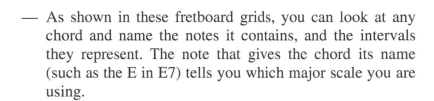

— Do the same process with up-the-neck moveable chords (chords that do not include open strings), like the barred C chord at right. (You will see chords like this in **ROADMAP #3**.)

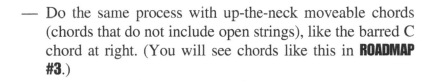

— **Learn the first-position major scales below.** They will make it easy for you to play melodies in the easy guitar keys (C, G, D, A, and E). Practice each scale by playing it over and over with a steady tempo.

C Major Scale

G Major Scale

D Major Scale

A Major Scale

E Major Scale

Even though a song has many chord changes, its melody can often be played using just one major scale: the major scale of the I chord. Try playing the melody to the cowboy folk song "Red River Valley," which is written below in five keys. In each key, the major scale of the I chord is all you need to play the tune. In all but the first key, C, some slides, hammer-ons, and pull-offs are used to slightly embellish the melody.

RED RIVER VALLEY

SUMMING UP—NOW YOU KNOW...

1. The intervals of the major scale (whole step, half step, etc.).

2. How to play a major scale on a single string.

3. The number of frets that make up each interval (a third, fourth, etc.).

4. How to find intervals on the fretboard in relation to the 6th and 5th strings.

5. How to recognize the key signatures, and how many sharps or flats are in each key.

6. How to analyze chords for notes and intervals.

7. How to play first-position major scales in the keys of C, G, D, A, and E.

8. The meaning of these musical terms:
   a) Intervals
   b) Key and key signature
   c) Chord
   d) Octave

TWO MOVEABLE MAJOR CHORD SHAPES

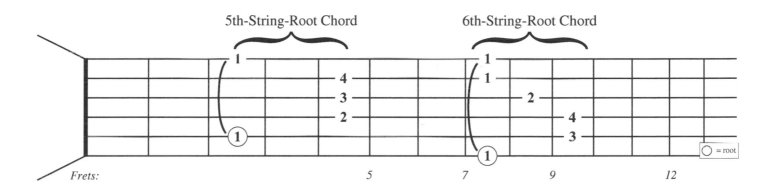

WHY? *Moveable chords* **have no open strings,** so they can be played (moved) all over the fretboard. The two moveable chords of **ROADMAP #3** will get you started playing chords up and down the neck. These two chord formations can be altered slightly to make dozens of chord types (minors, sevenths, ninths, etc.), so they are the foundation for the many chords you will learn in **ROADMAP #8**.

WHAT? **A moveable chord can be played all over the fretboard.** It contains no open (unfretted) strings.

A *root* **is the note that gives a chord its name.** The root of all C chords (C7, C minor, C augmented, etc.) is C.

A *major chord* **contains three notes:** the root, and the notes that are a third and a fifth above the root. For example, a C major chord consists of the 1st, 3rd, and 5th notes in the C major scale: C, E, and G.

The 6th-string-root chord formation is a "barred E" chord.
(Roots are circled.)

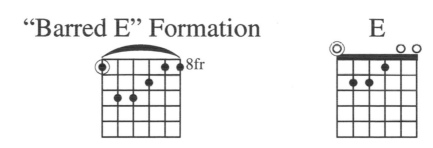

"Barred E" Formation   E

The 5th-string-root chord formation is a "barred A" chord.

"Barred A" Formation

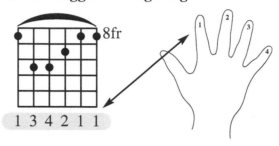

or

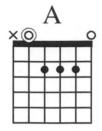

HOW? **Numbers under chord grids are suggested fingerings:**

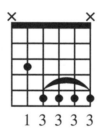

8fr

1 3 4 2 1 1

Barre the alternate 5th-string-root chord with your third or fourth finger, whichever is most comfortable. Most people can't help but fret the first string while doing this, but do not pick the first string with your strumming/picking hand.

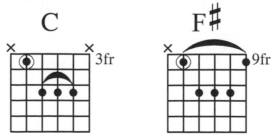

1 3 3 3 3

The 6th string identifies the 6th-string-root barred chord. It's a G chord when played at the 3rd fret, because the 6th string/3rd fret is G. At the 6th fret it's a B♭ chord, and so on.

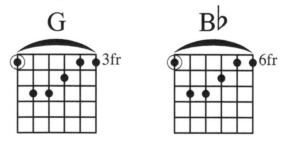

The 5th string identifies the 5th-string-root barred chord. It's a C chord at the 3rd fret, because the 5th string/3rd fret is C. At the 9th fret it's F♯ (G♭), and so on.

DO IT!   **Play the 6th-string-root chords all over the fretboard,** naming the chords as you play them.

Play the 5th-string-root chords all over the fretboard and name them.

Play any chord you can think of two ways:

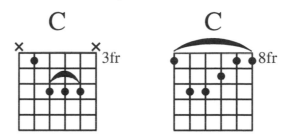

Play this rock progression* using 6th-string-root chords. It matches "Louie, Louie," "Twist and Shout," "La Bamba," "Wild Thing," "Good Lovin'," and many more classic rock tunes.

Key of G

This progression is divided into *measures*, with four beats to a measure. (Strum once for each beat.) The repeat signs ‖:   :‖ tell you to repeat the two measures of music, or any music enclosed within them.

*A *progression* is an ordered sequence of chords (usually with some relationship to each other), repeated many times within a song.

Play the same progression using 5th-string-root chords.

Key of G

Play it in different keys. This is easy if you observe the fret distances (intervals) between chords. For example, the second chord (C) in the progression is five frets above the first chord (G). This is true in all keys; the third chord is two frets above the second chord in any key.

Key of F

Key of C

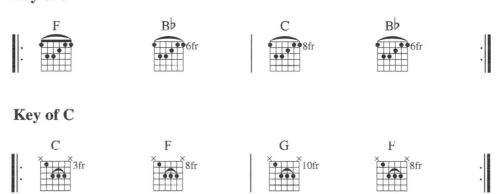

Play this basic rock progression, first with 6th-string-root chords, then with 5th-string-root chords:

Key of G

Play the same progression in other keys. Remember to look at the intervals between chords (e.g., the second chord is two frets below the first chord, etc.):

Key of C

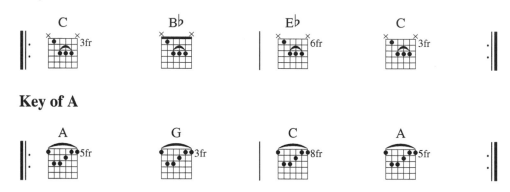

Key of A

Play this progression, first with 6th-string-root chords, then with 5th-string-root chords:

Key of G

Play the same progression in many different keys.

SUMMING UP—NOW YOU KNOW...

1. Two moveable chords, one with a 6th-string root, one with a 5th-string root.

2. How to play any major chord two ways, using the moveable major chords.

3. How to play simple progressions in all keys, using these chords.

4. The intervals that make up a major chord.

5. The meaning of these musical terms:
   a) Root
   b) Major Chord
   c) Progression

THE I–IV–V CHORD FAMILY

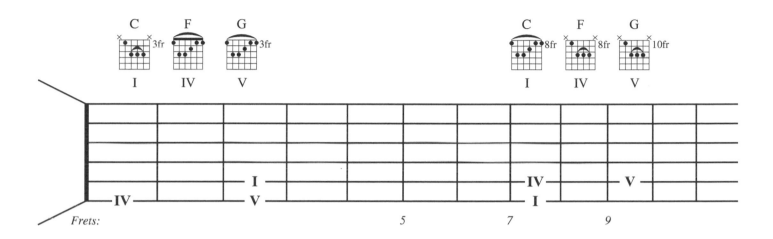

WHY? The **I–IV–V chord family** is the basis for countless chord progressions in pop, rock, country, blues, folk, and jazz. **ROADMAP #4** shows how to locate chord families automatically, in any key, all over the fretboard.

WHAT? The Roman numerals in the chart above are the roots of the I, IV, and V chords in the key of C.

The numerals I, IV, and V refer to the major scale of your key.

The I chord is so named because its root is the keynote, e.g., in the key of C, the C chord is the I chord.

The IV chord's root is a fourth above the keynote (a fourth above the root of the I chord). For example, F is the fourth note in the C major scale, so the F chord is the IV chord in the key of C.

The V chord's root is a fifth above the keynote. Its root is also a whole step above the root of the IV chord. G is a fifth above C (and a whole step above F), so the G chord is the V chord in the key of C.

The I, IV, and V chords form a "chord family." They are used together so frequently that in order to orient yourself to a given key, you must first locate them on the fretboard in that key.

HOW?   The I–IV–V root patterns in the fretboard chart are moveable.

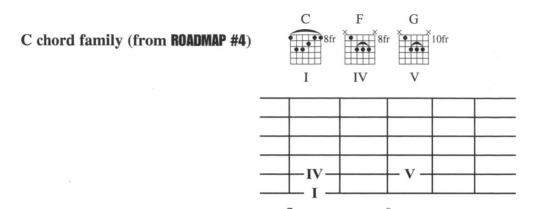

C chord family (from ROADMAP #4)

— The above C chord family has a 6th-string-root I chord.

— When the I chord has a 6th-string root, the IV chord's root is always on the same fret/5th string.

— The root of the V chord is always two frets above the IV chord's root.

— Here are some sample chord families that illustrate this pattern (roots are circled):

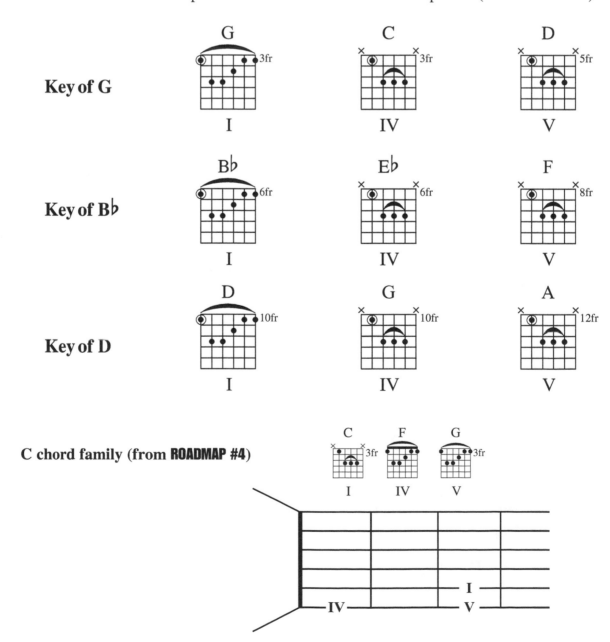

Key of G

Key of B♭

Key of D

C chord family (from ROADMAP #4)

— This C chord family has a 5th-string root.

— When the I chord has a 5th-string root, the root of the V chord is always on the same fret/6th string.

— The root of the IV chord is always two frets below that of the V chord. For example:

Key of F

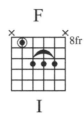
F
I

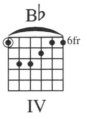
B♭
IV

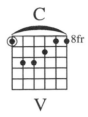
C
V

Key of D

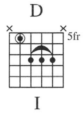
D
I

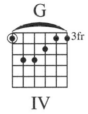
G
IV

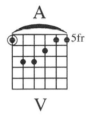
A
V

Key of G

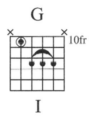
G
I

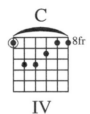
C
IV

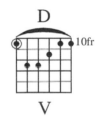
D
V

DO IT!   **Play several chord families two ways:** first with a 6th-string-root I chord, then with a 5th-string-root I chord. Here are two examples:

Key of E♭

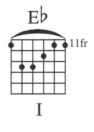
E♭
I

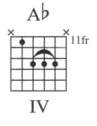
A♭
IV

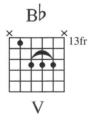
B♭
V

or

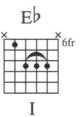
E♭
I

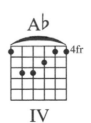
A♭
IV

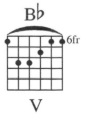
B♭
V

Key of A

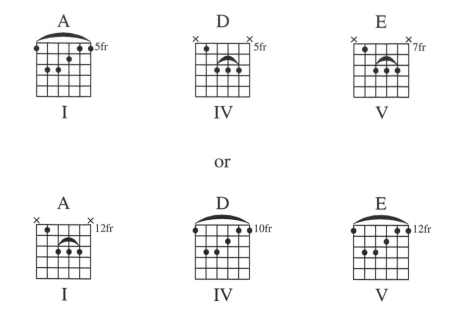

or

Play several common I–IV–I–V progressions in many different keys, with a 6th-string-root I chord and with a 5th-string-root I chord. For example, here is the basic rock "Louie Louie-esque" chord sequence:

$$\|\!: \quad I \quad IV \quad | \quad V \quad IV \quad :\|$$

The repeat signs $\|\!:$ $:\|$ tell you to repeat the two bars of music (or any music enclosed within them).

— Strum the pattern over and over in several keys, such as:

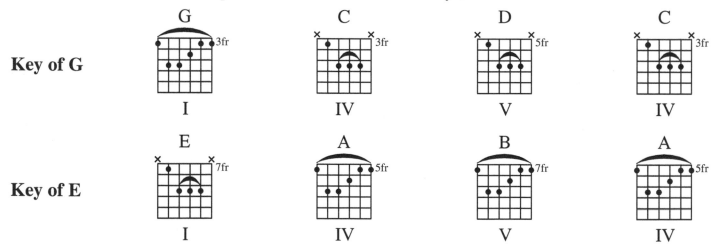

Key of G

Key of E

Play the same "tune" using the other G chord family (with a 5th-string-root I chord) and other E chord family (with a 6th-string-root I chord).

12-Bar Blues: This very important progression is the basis of many rock, blues, country, folk, and jazz tunes:

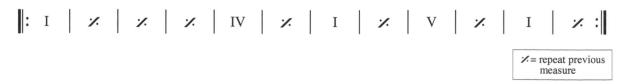

⁒ = repeat previous measure

— Play it in several keys using 5th- and 6th-string-root I chords. Here it is in G, with a 6th-string-root I chord:

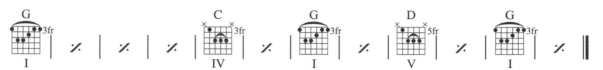

— As you strum the 12-bar blues in several keys, sing or hum these well-known tunes: "Kansas City," "Route 66," "Hound Dog," "Johnny B. Goode," "Blue Suede Shoes," "The Seventh Son," "Whole Lotta Shakin' Going On," "Rock Around the Clock," and "Stormy Monday."

Boogie-Woogie Lick: This backup lick that is so fundamental to blues and rock is based on the two moveable chords of **ROADMAP #3** and the chord families of **ROADMAP #4**. The barred chords are abbreviated to two- and three-note formations, and the little finger of your fretting hand adds extra, alternating (on-and-off) notes:

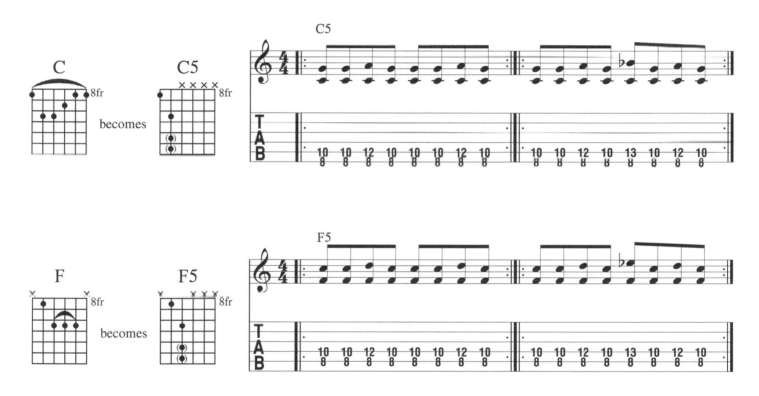

The abbreviated chords have a "5" in their names (C5, F5) because they consist of a root and fifth, but no third. This makes them different from most major chords. (See **ROADMAP #3** on the composition of a major chord.)

Use the Boogie-Woogie Lick as a backup for the 12-bar blues. Strum and hum "Kansas City," "Route 66," and the other 12-bar blues tunes you played before, but use abbreviated chords and add the boogie-woogie lick. Do it in different keys, starting with a 6th-string-root I chord and with a 5th-string-root I chord.

Here's a sample boogie-woogie backup part for a 12-bar rock/blues in the key of C. This accompaniment style is still used in rock, blues, and country.

Many rock tunes use the ♭III and ♭VII chords, in addition to the I, IV, and V. You can find the ♭III and ♭VII easily by relating them to the I chord:

— The ♭III chord is three frets *above* the I chord.

— The ♭VII chord is two frets *below* the I chord.

The fretboard diagrams below illustrate these root relationships:

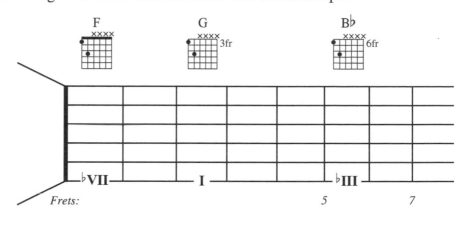

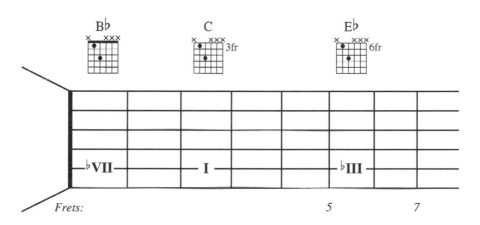

Here are some typical rock progressions that include the ♭III and ♭VII. Each is written with Roman numeral/roots and with chord grids, in the key of C. Play them in many keys.

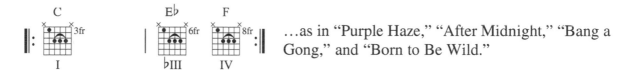

...as in "Purple Haze," "After Midnight," "Bang a Gong," and "Born to Be Wild."

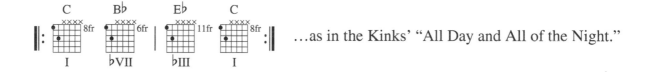

...as in the Kinks' "All Day and All of the Night."

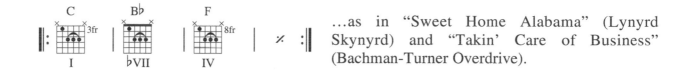

...as in "Sweet Home Alabama" (Lynyrd Skynyrd) and "Takin' Care of Business" (Bachman-Turner Overdrive).

Other rock tunes made of I, IV, and V chords plus the ♭III and ♭VII include "Bad Medicine" (Bon Jovi), "Dude Looks Like a Lady" (Aerosmith), "Hot Blooded" (Foreigner), "I Want Action" (Poison), and "Once Bitten Twice Shy" (Great White).

No matter what key you're in, going from I to IV or I to V has a recognizable sound. Once you train your ear to recognize the sound of the I chord moving to the IV or V chord, it becomes much easier to hear, understand, and play songs in any key.

Playing a familiar song in many different keys helps you learn to *hear* chord changes in terms of intervals. Try it with a simple, three-chord folk tune like "Midnight Special." While you strum the first-position chords that are indicated below, be aware that you're going to the V chord or the IV chord, and listen for the sound of each chord change.

MIDNIGHT SPECIAL

Key of C

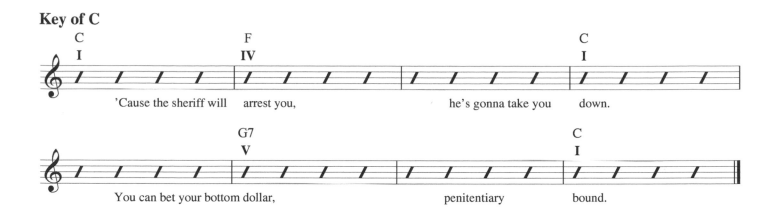

C — I
F — IV
C — I

'Cause the sheriff will arrest you,   he's gonna take you down.

G7 — V
C — I

You can bet your bottom dollar,   penitentiary bound.

SUMMING UP—NOW YOU KNOW...

1. Two different ways to play the I–IV–V chord family—in any key: with a 6th-string-root I chord and with a 5th-string-root I chord.

2. How to play the 12-bar blues and the "Louie Louie" progression in any key, two ways.

3. How to play the rock/blues boogie woogie lick in any key.

4. How to find the ♭III and ♭VII chords and use them in rock progressions—in any key.

5. The meaning of these musical terms:
    a) I chord
    b) IV chord
    c) V chord
    d) ♭III chord
    e) ♭VII chord
    f) Chord Family
    g) 12-Bar Blues
    h) Boogie-Woogie Backup

THE D—A—F ROADMAP

D Chords

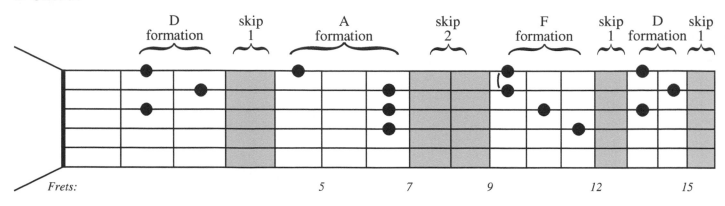

| | D formation | skip 1 | A formation | skip 2 | F formation | skip 1 | D formation | skip 1 |

WHY? The **D—A—F ROADMAP** shows you how to play any major chord all over the fretboard, using three major chord formations. It is especially useful when a tune stays on the same chord for a few measures, because it enables you to automatically "climb the fretboard," playing rapidly ascending or descending licks and *arpeggios.**

HOW? The chords in **ROADMAP #5** above are all D chords.

Here are the three major chord shapes used in this roadmap. Because they are played on the top three or four strings, they are sometimes called "chord fragments." The root of each is circled:

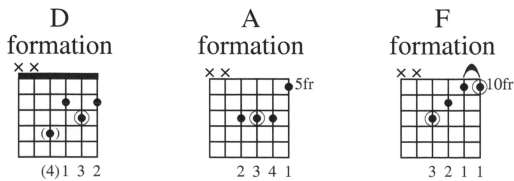

The (4) in the D formation (4th string/4th finger) is in parentheses because it is an optional note. The top three strings alone comprise a major chord.

The A formation is a variation of the basic, first-position A major chord:

*Playing an *arpeggio* is picking each note of a chord in succession, going up or down the strings, in a harp-like fashion:

HOW?

Here's how to use the D–A–F ROADMAP to play all the D chords:

— Play the first-position D chord, as shown in the main **ROADMAP #5** diagram.

— Skip a fret (the 4th, shaded fret) and play the A form. You are still playing a D chord, but you are fingering a different formation.

— Skip two frets (the shaded frets) and play the F form. This is the next, higher D chord.

— Skip one fret and play the D chord form again. It is still a higher D chord, an octave above your starting point.

— Continue the process (skip one fret and play the A chord form, skip two frets and play the F chord form) until you run out of frets.

To memorize this roadmap, remember: D–SKIP 1, A–SKIP 2, F–SKIP 1.

Use the D–A–F ROADMAP to play all the F chords:

F Chords

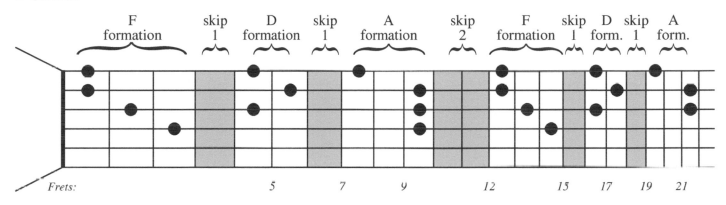

Notice that you can climb the fretboard *starting with any chord formation*. The **D–A–F ROADMAP** is a continuous loop that you can enter at any point. It can be the **A–F–D ROADMAP**, or the **F–D–A ROADMAP**. The "skips" are always the same: one skip after D, two after A, and one after F.

To emphasize that point, here are all the C chords, starting with the A formation/C chord. Now the roadmap is **A–F–D**.

C Chords

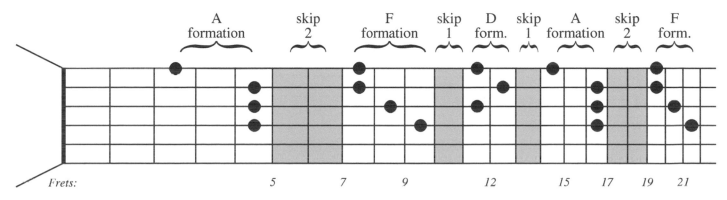

DO IT! Here are some practical applications of the **D–A–F ROADMAP**. To learn the diagram, say or think "D–skip one, A–skip 2, F–skip 1" while playing the ascending chords. Name the formations as you play them.

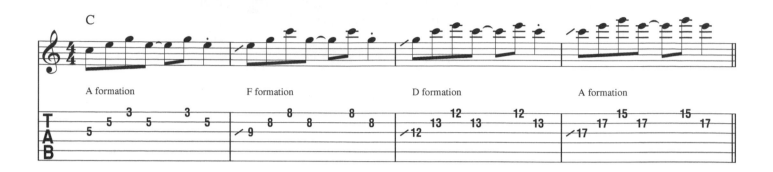

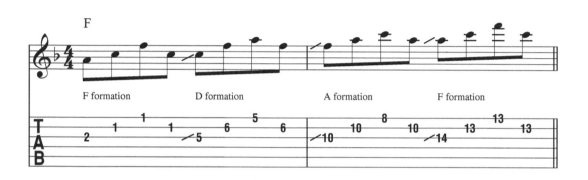

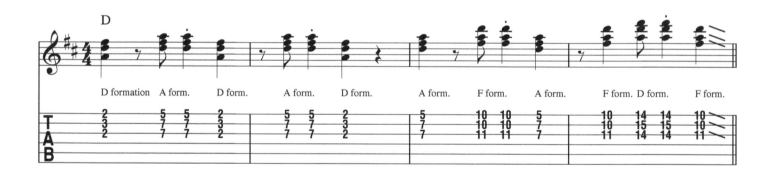

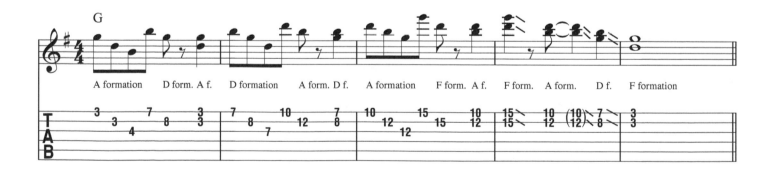

Play each exercise in different keys and make up similar patterns. Your ear will tell you if you are using the roadmap correctly, because within any one exercise the ascending or descending chord forms should all sound like the *same chord*.

You can alter the three major D, A, and F chord fragments slightly to create many different chords. The chart below indicates notes that are adjacent to each of the three chord fragments (the numbers indicate intervals). Countless licks can be created by adding these notes to arpeggios, or hammering onto them or pulling off from them.*

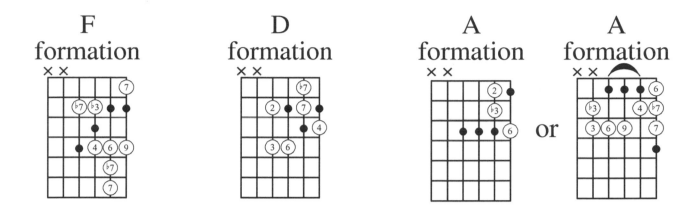

These chord variations are the basis of a lead guitar style that is used by rock, country, and R&B players.

*To *hammer on* to a note, pick the note below it, and "hammer" the note with another finger. To *pull off*, reverse the process: play the higher note, and pull your finger off to sound the lower note.

The following examples are all licks in the key of G. They make use of all three chord fragments and their variations.

F-formation licks

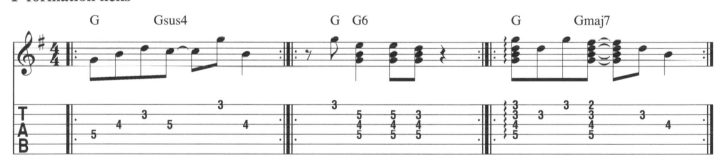

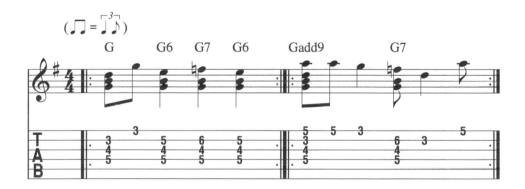

D-formation licks

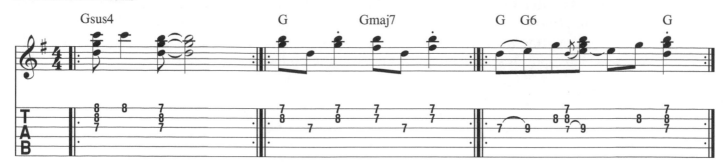

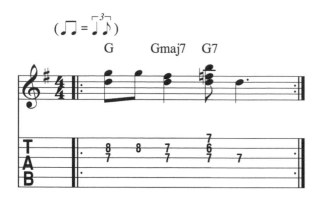

A-formation licks

All these variations can make your D–A–F ascending and descending licks more interesting.
Here is an example with an ascending G chord:

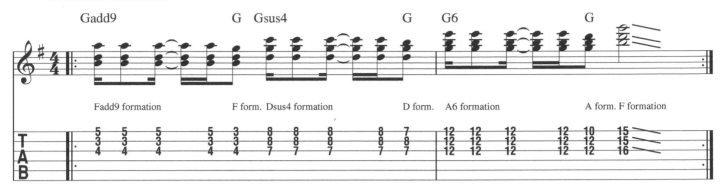

All three major chord shapes can be altered slightly to create minor and 7th chords:

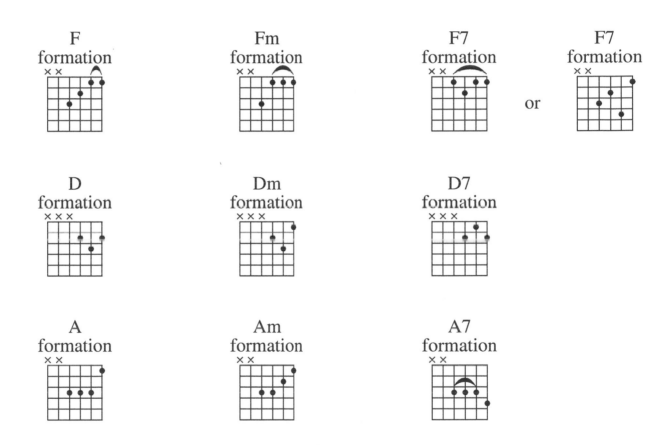

Here are the minor and seventh versions of the D–A–F ROADMAP:

Dm Chords

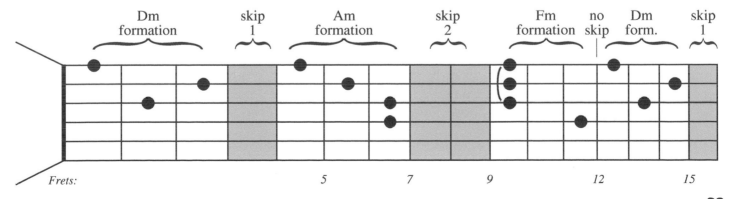

D7 Chords

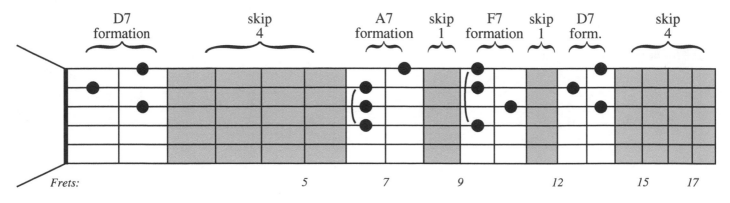

SUMMING UP—NOW YOU KNOW...

1. How to play three major chord fragments.

2. How to use them to play any major chord all over the fretboard (with the **D–A–F ROADMAP**).

3. How to alter them to play many licks.

4. How to play licks that stay on one chord but go all over the fretboard with and without 6ths, 7ths, and other variations.

5. How to alter the three major chord fragments to make them minor and seventh chords.

6. The meaning of these musical terms:
    a) Arpeggio
    b) Hammer-on
    c) Pull-off

CHORD FRAGMENT/ CHORD FAMILIES

Three B♭ chord families:

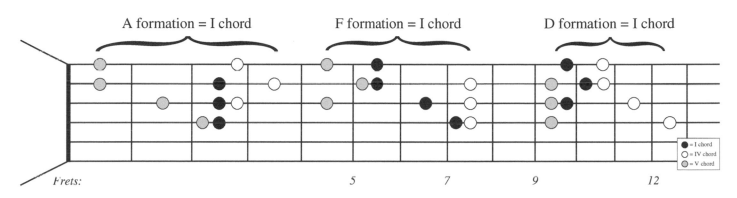

WHY? This chart arranges the three chord fragments of **ROADMAP #5** into chord families to help you play chords and chord-based licks all over the fretboard in *any key*. You can move automatically from I to IV to V in three different places on the guitar (per key) using the same three- or four-note chord fragments you played in **ROADMAP #5**.

WHAT? **You can play at least three chord families for every key:**

— A chord family with an F-formation I chord:

— A chord family with a D-formation I chord:

— A chord family with an A-formation I chord:

The A formation can look like this:

or this (barred with the index finger):

The fret relationships within each chord family are *fixed***.** That is, if you play an F-formation I chord, the V chord is the D formation one fret lower—in any key. For example:

Key of A

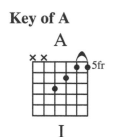
A
I

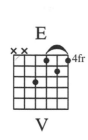
E
V

Key of C

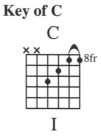
C
I

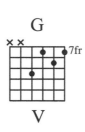
G
V

Key of D

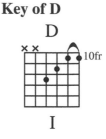
D
I

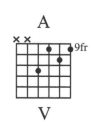
A
V

You can locate the three chord families for any key by placing the root of the I chords in the appropriate places:

I chords in the key of F (roots circled)

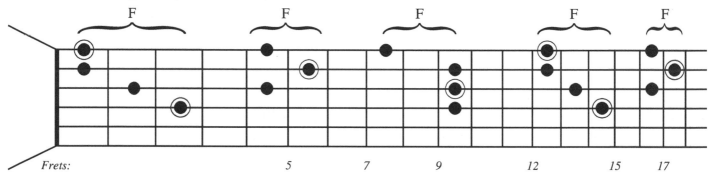

Frets: 5 7 9 12 15 17

You can find these I chords "automatically" once you have memorized the **D–A–F ROADMAP (#5)**.

You can play backup licks and solos by picking arpeggios on the chord fragments (see the **DO IT!** section that follows).

HOW? **Learn the relationships of the three chord fragment/chord families** and you can make quick chord changes automatically. For example, if you're playing a *I chord* with an F formation, the *IV chord* is the A formation on the same three frets.

DO IT! **Here are some typical chord fragment/chord family licks. They will give you some practice memorizing the chord family relationships.** They are all in the key of G and have a I–IV–V (G–C–D) chord progression. In several of them you strum the chord fragments, and in some you play arpeggios. Play each two- or four-measure pattern over and over:

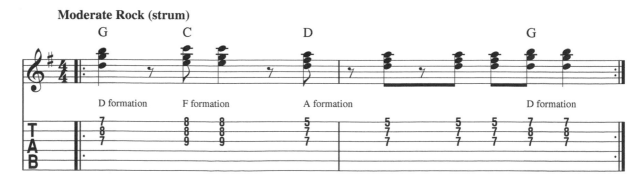

36

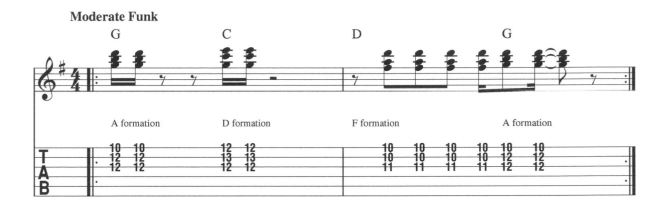

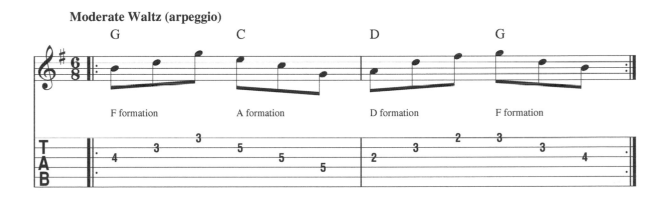

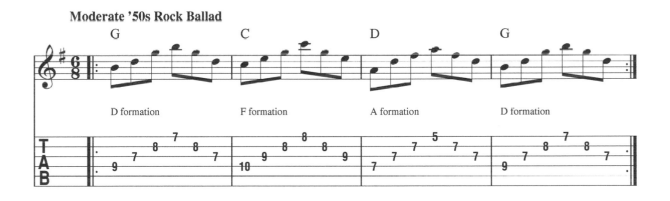

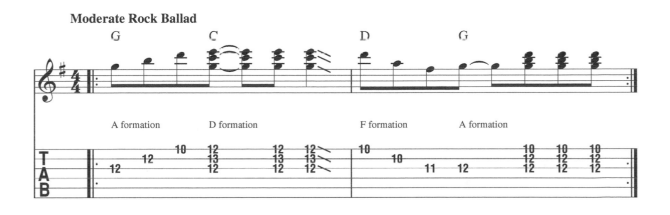

The following chord fragment/chord family licks are in the key of C and have I–IV–V (C–F–G) chord progressions. They make use of the chord fragment variations (7th chords, suspended chords, etc.), as well as the standard F, D, and A chord fragments.

Moderate Rock

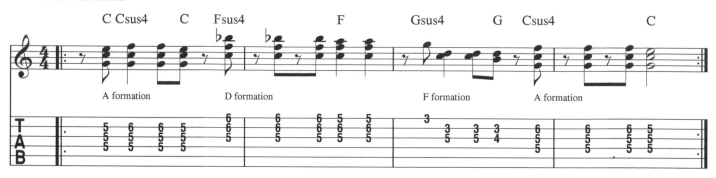

Moderate Country

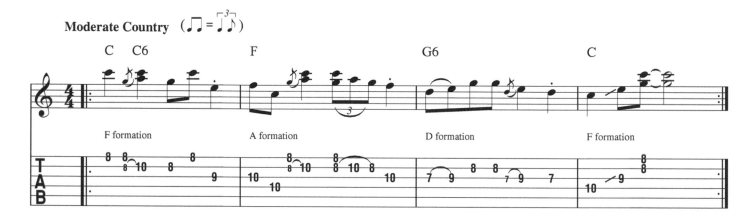

Moderate Rock Ballad

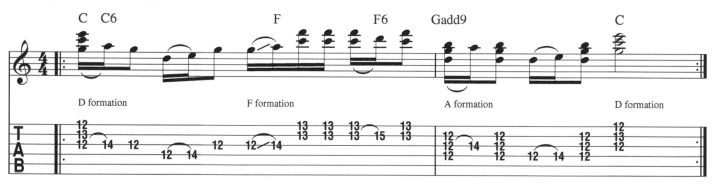

Moderate Folk-Rock

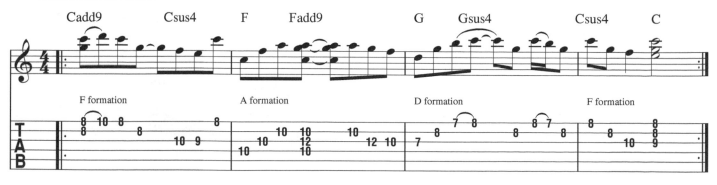

The IV chord two frets higher = the V chord, so you can enlarge all three chord fragments/chord families. Now you have two V chords from which to choose:

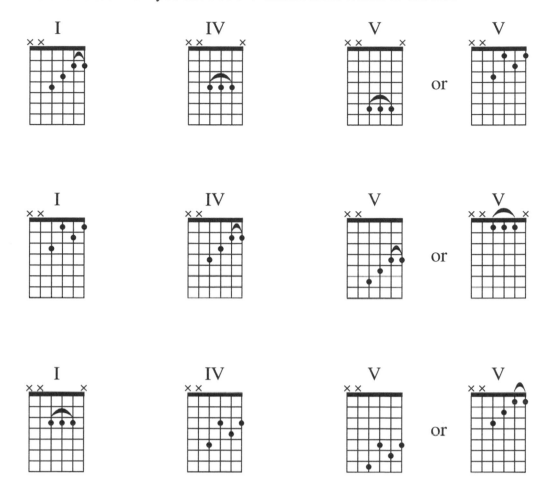

Play these brief I–IV–V phrases. They make use of the V chord, which is a IV chord moved up two frets:

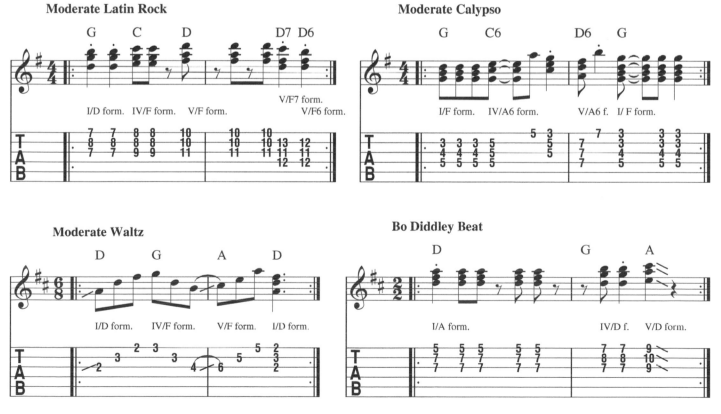

The reverse is also true: the V chord two frets lower = the IV chord. So you have two IV chords from which to choose in each chord fragment/chord family. For example:

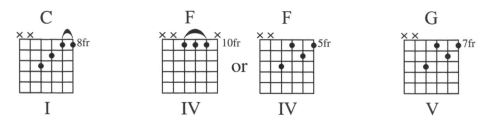

Here are some I–IV–V phrases that illustrate this chord relationship:

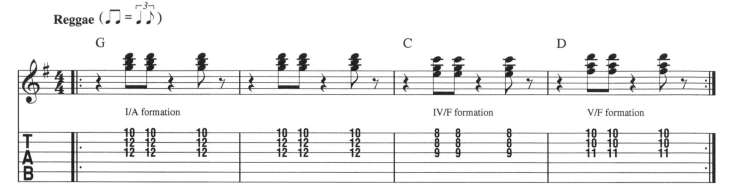

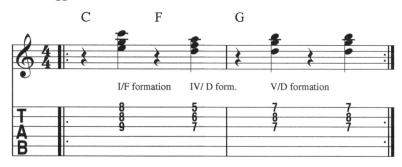

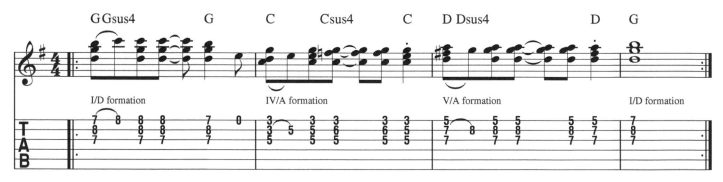

SUMMING UP—NOW YOU KNOW...

1. How to locate three different chord families for any key, using chord fragments.

2. How to play many licks, strum patterns, and arpeggios, using all three chord fragment/chord families, with or without chord variations.

3. How to expand the three chord families to include an alternate IV and V chord.

40

CIRCLE-OF-FIFTHS PROGRESSIONS

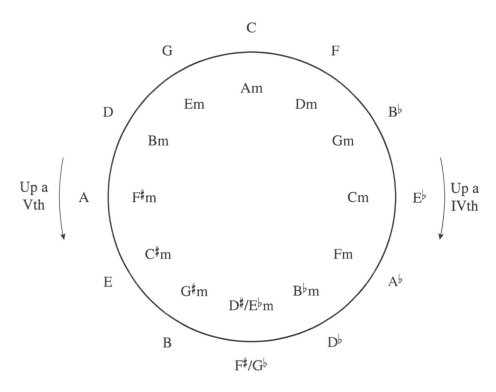

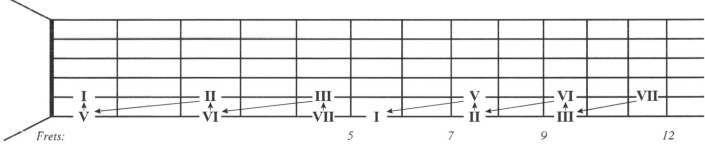

WHY? An understanding of the circle of fifths, combined with this root pattern diagram, makes it easy to play many frequently-used chord progressions automatically, in any key.

WHAT? The circle-of-fifths (also called the "circle-of-fourths") arranges the twelve musical notes so that **a step counter-clockwise takes you up a fifth, and a step clockwise takes you up a fourth**.

— **Counter-clockwise:** G is a fifth above C, B a fifth above E, etc.

— **Clockwise:** F is a fourth above C, B♭ is a fourth above F, etc.

— **This arrangement makes chord families visual:** If C is your I chord, F (IV) is next to it on the right, and G (V) is next to it on the left. The next chords out are D (II) and B♭ (♭VII), the two next-most-likely-to-occur chords in the key of C, other than relative minors.

41

Relative minors **are inside the circle** (e.g., Am is the relative minor to C). The relative minor chord is a minor 3rd (three frets) below its relative major. The two chords contain most of the same notes and are closely related (the A minor scale contains the same notes as the C major scale).

If I, IV, and V chords make up the immediate family, their relative minors are the extended family. They are often used in common chord progressions. Thus, in the key of C: C (I), F (IV), and G (V) are an immediate family, and the relative minors are Am (relative minor to C), Dm (relative to F), and Em (relative to G).

Transposing: *Transposition* means changing a song's key. The circle diagram is a useful tool that can help you transpose. For instance, if you find a tune written out in a songbook in E♭ or D♭, you can change it to a more guitar-friendly key (C, G, D, A, or E) by looking at the distance on the circle between the given key and your key. C is three counter-clockwise steps away from E♭ on the circle, so to transpose from E♭ to C you move every chord in the tune three counter-clockwise steps. A♭ becomes F, Cm becomes Am, B♭ becomes G, etc. This is also helpful when you accompany a singer, because it's often necessary to change keys to accommodate a vocalist's range.

HOW? Circle-of-fifths progressions: Thousands of songs of all genres (rock, jazz, country, blues, etc.) are based on circle-of-fifths motion. **In circle-of-fifths progressions, you leave the I chord (creating tension) and come back to I (resolving tension) by clockwise motion,** going up by 4ths until you are "home" at the I chord. For example, in the following key-of-C progression, you jump from C to A7 (leaving the C chord family), and then get back to C by going clockwise along the circle: D7 is a 4th above A, G7 is a 4th above D7, and C is a 4th above G7.

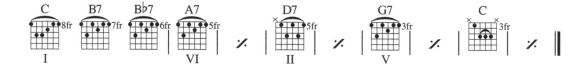

Many tunes have this **VI–II–V–I** (or **I–VI–II–V**) progression, including "Up a Lazy River," "Sweet Georgia Brown," "Salty Dog," and "Alice's Restaurant." The "walk down" from I to VI that starts all these tunes is a signal that you're about to hear a VI–II–V–I progression.

As you move clockwise along the circle, the chords can be major or minor, but the V chord is almost always a 7th. In another very common circle-of-fifths progression, the VI and II chords are minor (written as "vi" and "ii"). In the key of C:

This progression is so common that pros have nicknamed it "standard changes," "the dime-store progression," "ice cream changes," "rhythm changes," etc. It's the basis for countless thirties and forties standards ("Blue Moon," "Heart and Soul," "These Foolish Things," "I Got Rhythm"), fifties and sixties classic rock tunes ("Oh Donna," "You Send Me," "Stand by Me," "Sincerely," "Be My Baby"), and more recent pop and rock songs ("Every Time You Go Away," "Every Breath You Take," "[Everybody Has a] Hungry Heart").

In many I–vi–ii–V progressions, IV is substituted for ii, which changes the progression to I–vi–IV–V, or, in the key of C: C–Am–F–G7. It's a subtle change, because IV and ii are very similar chords; ii is the relative minor to IV (e.g., in the key of C, Dm is the relative minor to F).

C (I) – Am (vi) – F (IV) – G7 (V)

ii–V–I is the basis for many tunes, and is also a "turnaround" (a two- or four-measure phrase at the end of a verse or chorus that sets up a repeat of the verse or chorus). "Satin Doll," "El Paso," "My Sweet Lord" and "Honeysuckle Rose" are based on ii–V–I.

III–VI–II–V–I progressions go a step farther back on the circle:

E7 (III) – A7 (VI) – D7 (II) – G7 (V) – C (I)

This is the famous "I Got Rhythm" bridge, which occurs as a bridge in many tunes. It is also the basis for many standards like "All of Me" and "Please Don't Talk About Me When I'm Gone." Sometimes the III, VI, or II is minor.

VII–III–VI–II–V–I cycles back even farther, to the VII chord:

B7 (VII) – E7 (III) – A7 (VI) – D7 (II) – G7 (V) – C (I)

"Mister Sandman" and "Red Roses for a Blue Lady" are two examples.

Circle-of-fifths movement on the fretboard follows a zig-zag pattern:

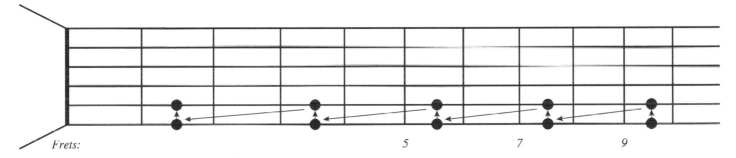

Frets: 5 7 9

— Starting with a 6th-string root note, you go up a fourth (one step clockwise on the circle) by going up a string to the 5th string/same fret (e.g., from C, 6th string/8th fret, to F, 5th string/8th fret).

— Starting with a 5th-string root note, you get to the root of the IV chord (one step clockwise on the circle) by going down a string to the 6th string/two frets lower (e.g., from F, 5th string/8th fret, to B♭, 6th string/6th fret).

— Thus, you play circle-of-fifths progressions when you follow the zig-zag chart above, assigning chords to each root note. For example, you could play a VII–III–VI–II–V–I progression in D♭ like this, starting from the VII chord:

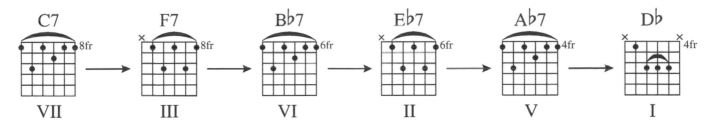

Or, with some minor chords:

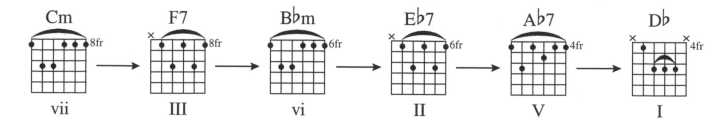

Cm	F7	B♭m	E♭7	A♭7	D♭
vii	III	vi	II	V	I

DO IT! Just as the I–IV–V root patterns of **ROADMAP #4** help you locate chord families automatically on the fretboard, so **ROADMAP #7** helps you play circle-of-fifths chord movement. In both diagrams, you play chords based on the root notes that are pictured on the fretboard.

— ii–V–I: Play these ii–V–I phrases in the key of B♭. They have a 5th-string-root I chord:

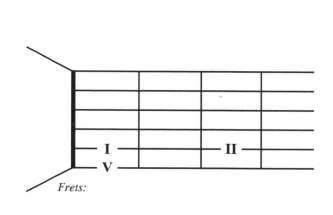

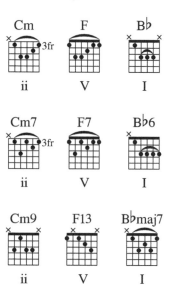

— These ii–V– I phrases in B♭ have a 6th-string-root I chord:

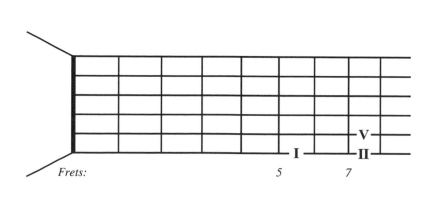

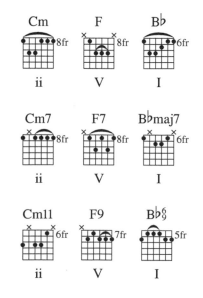

The lowest note in each of the above chords is its root, and all the ii–V–I progressions above follow the zig-zag fretboard root patterns of **ROADMAP #7**. For more information about the chord formations, see **ROADMAP #8**.

Relative Minors: These can be found automatically. Look at **ROADMAP #7** and you'll see these root patterns:

6th-string-root I chord – Key of A

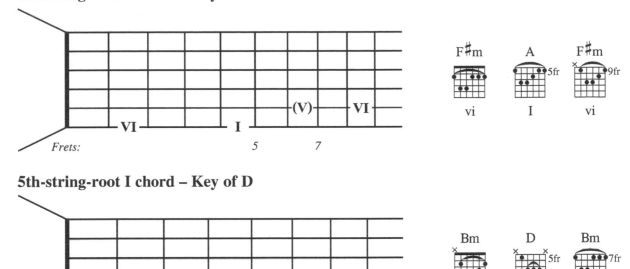

5th-string-root I chord – Key of D

As the fretboard root-pattern charts above indicate, there are two ways to find the relative minor. Both ways work for a 6th-string-root I chord and a 5th-string-root I chord:

— Play a minor chord whose root is three frets lower than the root of the I chord.

— Play a minor chord whose root is two frets higher than the root of the V chord (vi is two frets above V).

Practice finding relative minors. Play random major chords with 5th- and 6th-string roots and find two relative minors for each major chord, like this:

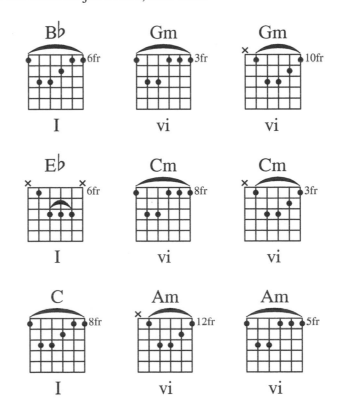

I–vi–ii–V: To play this popular progression, you jump from the I chord to the vi chord and zig-zag back to I. Play these examples and sing along with your favorites from the list of "standard changes" songs on page 42:

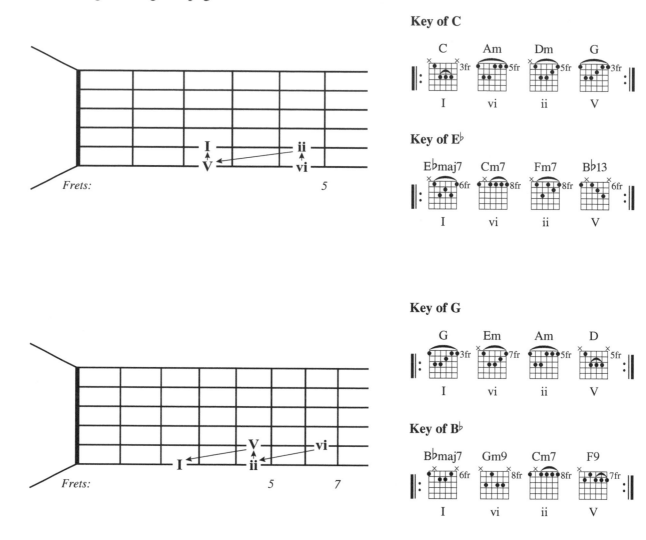

III–VI–II–V–I and **VII–III–VI–II–V–I:** Do some serious zig-zagging and play these sample progressions:

5th-string-root I chord – Key of B♭

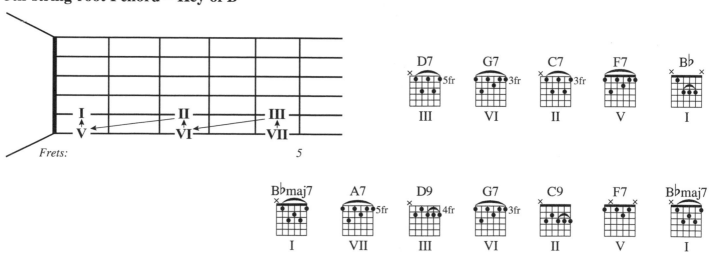

6th-string-root I chord – Key of F

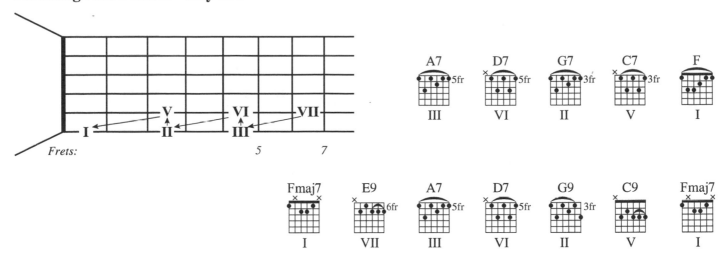

SUMMING UP—NOW YOU KNOW...

1. How to play several circle-of-fifths progressions in any key using the "zig-zag" method.

2. How to locate relative minor chords on the fretboard.

3. How to transpose.

4. Several standard chord progressions, including the "standard changes" and the "I Got Rhythm" bridge

5. The meaning of these musical terms:
    a) Circle-of-fifths
    b) Relative minor
    c) Relative major
    d) Transposing

VARIATIONS OF THE TWO MOVEABLE MAJOR CHORDS

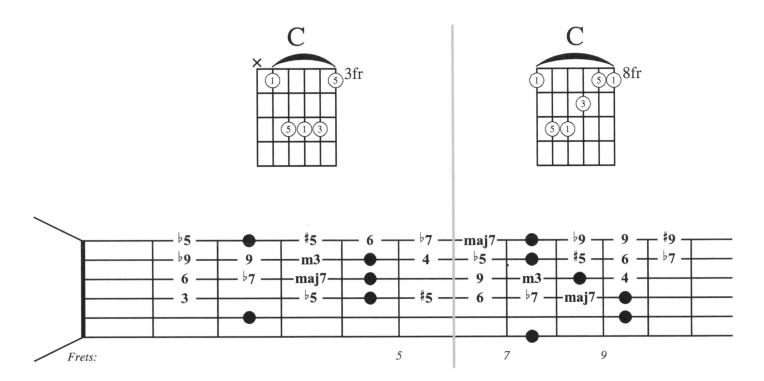

WHY? You can play dozens of chords (ninths, minor sevenths, major sevenths, etc.) by slightly altering the two basic, moveable major chords of **ROADMAP #3** (for example, you can play one fret lower on one string to make a major chord minor). This is an easy way to expand your chord vocabulary.

WHAT? **The two moveable major chords (and all major chords) consist of roots, 3rds, and 5ths.** Make sure you know the intervals in these two formations. The chord grids above **ROADMAP #8** identify the intervals (e.g., the 5th and 2nd strings in the barred E formation are 5ths).

You can relate other intervals (4ths, 7ths, etc.) to 1, 3, and 5. For example, a 4th is one fret higher than a 3rd, and a 6th is two frets higher than a 5th.

Some new musical terms:

— **Augmented:** Raised a half tone (one fret) in pitch, usually in reference to the interval of a 5th in a chord.

— **Diminished:** Lowered a half tone (one fret) in pitch.

— **Suspended:** The 3rd in the 1–3–5 major chord is replaced by the fourth.

HOW? To know *how* to alter the two moveable major chords to create other chord types, you need to know the formulas for the different types. Most of these formulas are in the boxes that follow.

— Sometimes chord symbols in songbooks and fakebooks are self-explanatory. For example, G sixth is written G6 and G ninth is written G9. Other symbols can be unfamiliar or confusing. In the boxes below, each chord formula is followed by a "G" chord symbol (G7, G9, etc.) to show how the chord type is commonly written.

MAJOR CHORDS:

Major = 1, 3, 5 (G)
Sixth = 1, 3, 5, 6 (G6)
Major Seventh = 1, 3, 5, 7 (Gmaj7, GM7, GΔ7, GΔ)
Major Ninth = 1, 3, 5, 7, 9 (Gmaj9, GM9, GΔ9)
Add Nine = 1, 3, 5, 9 (Gadd9)
Six/Nine = 1, 3, 5, 6, 9 (G$^6_9$, G6/9)
Suspended = 1, 4, 5 (Gsus, Gsus4)
Augmented = 1, 3, $\sharp$5 (G+)

MINOR CHORDS:

Minor = 1, $\flat$3, 5 (Gm, G-)
Minor Sixth = 1, $\flat$3, 5, 6 (Gm6, G-6)
Minor Seventh = 1, $\flat$3, 5, $\flat$7 (Gm7, G-7)
Minor Ninth = 1, $\flat$3, 5, $\flat$7, 9 (Gm9)
Minor Six/Nine = 1, $\flat$3, 5, 6, 9 (Gm$^6_9$, Gm6/9)
Minor Seven/Flat Five = 1, $\flat$3, $\flat$5, $\flat$7 (Gm7$\flat$5, G$^\varnothing$) (G$^\varnothing$ reads "G half-diminished")
Minor Eleven = 1, $\flat$3, 5, $\flat$7, 11 (Gm11)
Minor/Major Seven = 1, $\flat$3, 5, 7 (Gm(maj7), GmΔ7)

DOMINANT SEVENTH CHORDS (Sevenths)

Seventh = 1, 3, 5, $\flat$7 (G7)
Ninth = 1, 3, 5, $\flat$7, 9 (G9)
Eleventh = 1, 3, 5, $\flat$7, 9, 11 (G11)
Thirteenth = 1, 3, 5, $\flat$7, 9, 13 (G13)

You can add to these four types by flatting or sharping (augmenting) 5ths and 9ths, adding a suspended 4th, etc.

Seventh/Flat Five = 1, 3, $\flat$5, $\flat$7 (G7$\flat$5)
Seventh Augmented = 1, 3, $\sharp$5, $\flat$7 (G+7)
Seventh Suspended = 1, 4, 5, $\flat$7 (G7sus4)
Seventh/Flat Nine = 1, 3, 5, $\flat$7, $\flat$9 (G7$\flat$9)
Seventh/Sharp Nine = 1, 3, 5, $\flat$7, $\sharp$9 (G7$\sharp$9)
Seventh/Flat Nine Augmented = 1, 3, $\sharp$5, $\flat$7, $\flat$9 (G+7$\flat$9, G7$^{\flat 9}_{\sharp 5}$)
Seventh/Sharp Nine Augmented = 1, 3, $\sharp$5, $\flat$7, $\sharp$9 (G+7$\sharp$9, G7$^{\sharp 9}_{\sharp 5}$)
Ninth/Augmented = 1, 3, $\sharp$5, $\flat$7, 9 (G+9, G9$\sharp$5)
Ninth/Flat Five = 1, 3, $\flat$5, $\flat$7, 9 (G9$\flat$5)
Eleventh Augmented = 1, 3, 5, $\flat$7, 9, $\sharp$11 (G9$\sharp$11)
Thirteenth = 1, 3, 5, $\flat$7, 9, 13 (G13)
Thirteenth/Flat Nine = 1, 3, 5, $\flat$7, $\flat$9, 13 (G13$\flat$9)

DIMINISHED = 1, $\flat$3, $\flat$5, $\flat\flat$7 ($\flat\flat$7 = 6) (Gdim, G$^\circ$)

DO IT! **Use ROADMAP #8 to create a 5th- and 6th-string-root chord for each chord type.** For example, the formula for a minor chord differs by only one note from the formula for a major chord:

— A major chord is 1, 3 and 5; you flat the 3rd to make the chord minor (1, ♭3, 5).

— To make the 6th- and 5th-string root major chords into minor chords, you lower the 3rd by one fret:

Major    minor

This is just like making a first-position E into an Em.

E 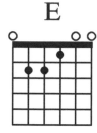   Em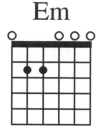

Major 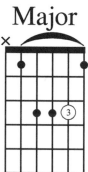   minor

This is just like making a first-position A into an Am.

A 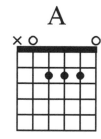   Am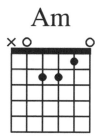

A dominant seventh chord has the same 1, 3, and 5 formula as a major chord, with a ♭7 added (1, 3, 5, ♭7).

— You remove a finger from the two moveable major chords to add the ♭7:

Major 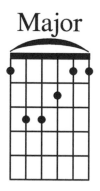   7th

This is just like making a first-position E into an E7.

E 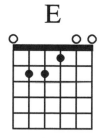   E7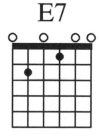

Major    7th

This is just like making a first-position A into an A7.

A 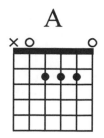   A7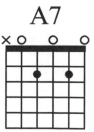

Minor seventh chords have a flatted third *and* a flatted seventh. The formula is 1, ♭3, 5, ♭7.

— To make the moveable major chords into minor sevenths, you make both of the above changes—a flatted third and a flatted seventh:

Make sure you know a 5th- and 6th-string-root chord for each chord type. Play both formations all over the fretboard to hear the sound of that chord type. For example, play the two major 7th formations like this:

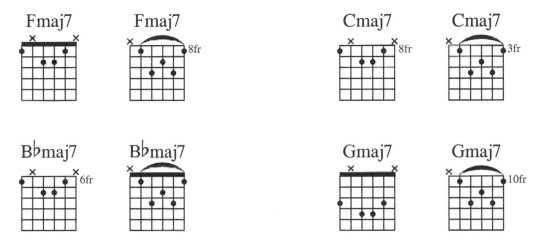

SAMPLE CHORD GRIDS FOR EACH CHORD TYPE

To make analysis of intervals easier, here are the formations divided into categories: major, minor, and dominant seventh chords. (M7 = major 7th.) Play each formation and analyze its intervals. Compare each small chord grid to the larger grid to its left, from which it is derived.

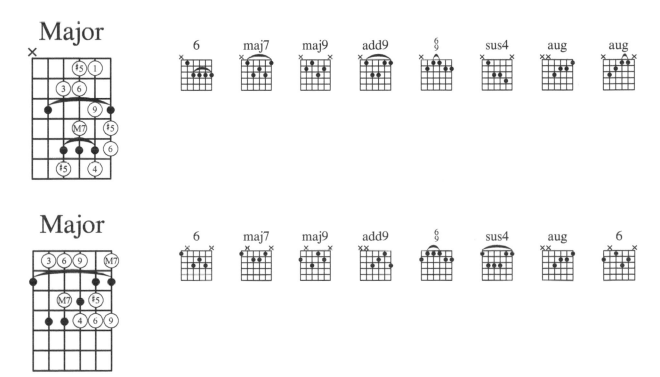

minor

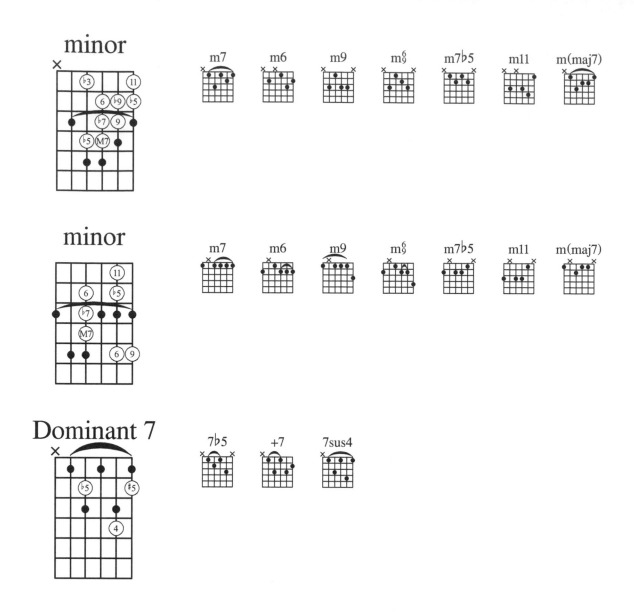

Dominant 7

Here is another very useful dominant seventh shape with a 5th-string root:

Dominant 7

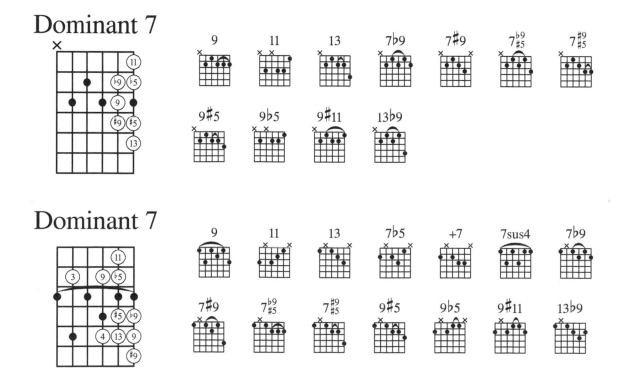

Diminished Chords

Dominant 7

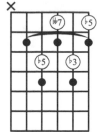

Dominant 7

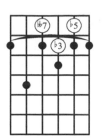

The **diminished chord** (1, ♭3, ♭5, ♭♭7) has some unusual characteristics:

It repeats every three frets. For example, these are all C diminished chords. Check for yourself: they all have the same four notes: C (1), E♭ (♭3), G♭ (♭5), and A (♭♭7).

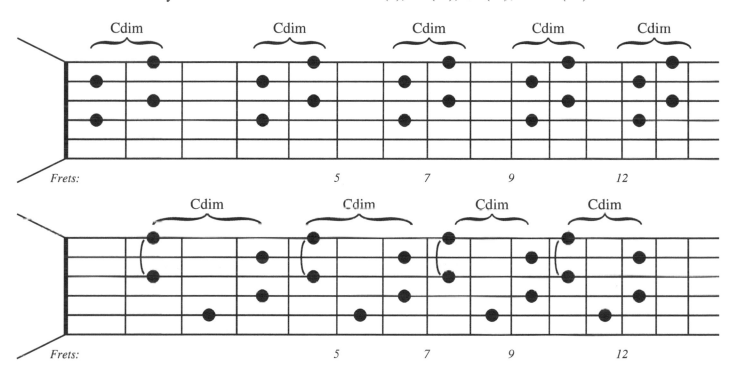

A diminished chord can be named by any of the four notes it contains. C diminished can also be called E♭ diminished, G♭ diminished, or A diminished, depending on the musical context in which it appears.

SUMMING UP—NOW YOU KNOW...

1. The formulas for many chord types.

2. Two ways to play each chord type—with a 5th-string root and a 6th-string root.

3. The meaning of these musical terms:
   a) Augmented
   b) Diminished
   c) Suspended

MOVEABLE MAJOR SCALES

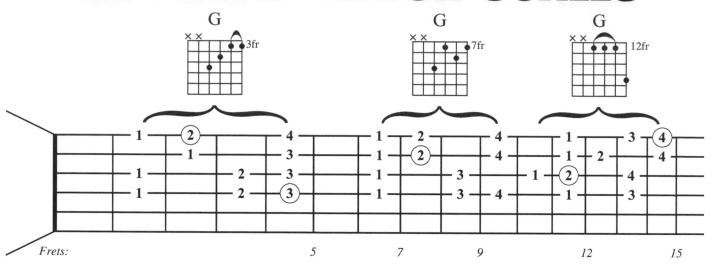

WHY? The major scale is the basis for countless melodies in tunes of many genres—rock, country, jazz, folk, and pop. Familiarity with several moveable major scales allows you to find and play melodies without memorizing them in advance. It brings you a step closer to any player's goal: to be able to *play* whatever you can hear.

WHAT? **The numbers on the fretboard in ROADMAP #9 are left-hand fingering suggestions.**

The three scales of ROADMAP #9 are based on the three chord fragments of ROADMAPS #5 and #6. The root notes (all Gs in this diagram) are circled. Play the appropriate chord fragment to get your fretting hand in position to play one of the major scales. For example, play an F formation at the 3rd fret to play the lowest G scale of **ROADMAP #9.**

This variation of **ROADMAP #9** shows the relationship between the scale patterns and their matching chord fragments:

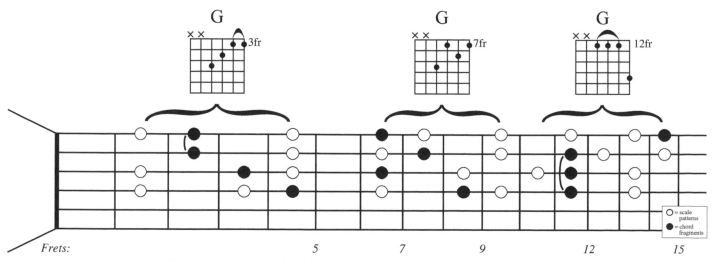

Occasionally, your left hand will move off the chord position as you play the major scales; the chord fragments are helpful frames of reference. Use the suggested left-hand fingering.

If you combine the information in **ROADMAPS #9** and **#5**, you have three ways to play any major scale. For example, in the key of C you can play the major scales associated with these three chord fragments:

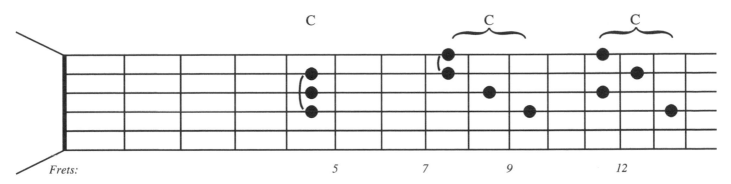

There are more major scale positions higher up the neck. They are the "twelve-frets-higher repeats" of the three basic positions. For example, in the key of F, you can repeat the F and D formation scales an octave higher:

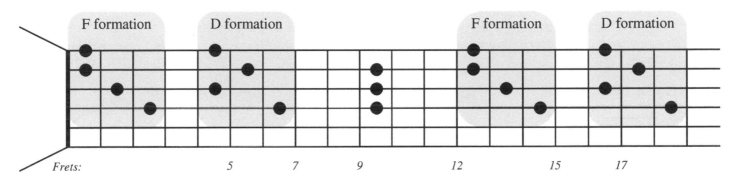

HOW?

Here are the three G scales that match the three G chord fragments. Play each one over and over. Get your left hand in position to play each scale by playing the chord fragment that matches it. Start each scale with its root note, so you can recognize the "do-re-mi" sound you have heard all your life!

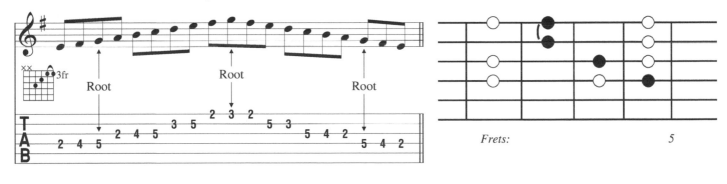

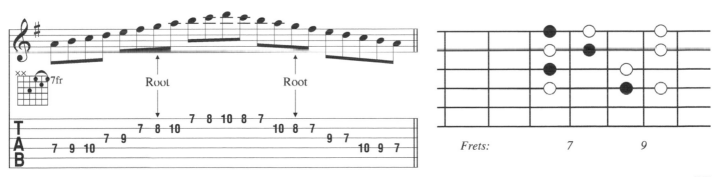

55

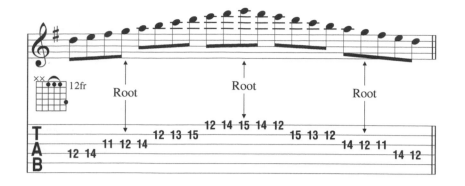 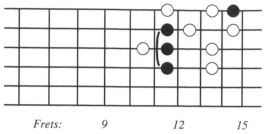

DO IT! **Become familiar with the scale patterns** by playing each scale over and over, in several places on the fretboard. Use the F-formation scale pattern to play G, A, C, D, and E major scales. Use the D formation pattern to play E, F, G, and A major scales. Use the A formation pattern to play B, C, D, E, and F scales.

Once you are familiar with a scale pattern, use it to play melodies. You can develop your ear and learn to play tunes by starting with simple familiar ones, such as nursery rhymes:

Mary Had a Little Lamb

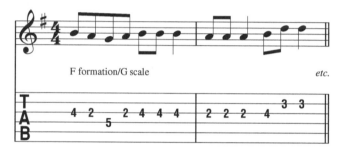

Twinkle, Twinkle, Little Star

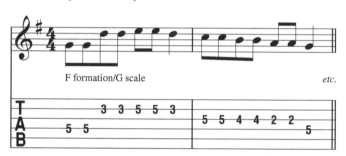

Try to play a melody using all three scale patterns. Some tunes can be played easily in two registers (i.e., high and low on the fretboard), using two different scale patterns. "Mary Had a Little Lamb" is written below, played with the D formation scale pattern. It can be played in the same register using the A pattern. The "Twinkle, Twinkle, Little Star" melody is too high for the D pattern, but can be played in the A pattern:

Mary Had a Little Lamb

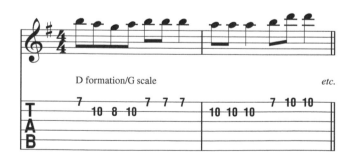

Twinkle, Twinkle, Little Star

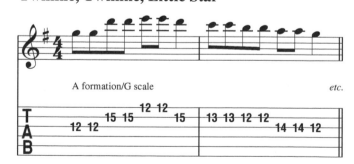

Play all kind of tunes and continue to develop your ear by searching for melodies. Use all three scale patterns and play in many keys. When you use moveable scales, there are no easy or difficult keys—they are all the same.

56

The major scale patterns can include all six strings. The previous four-string patterns can be extended to enable you to play melodies in lower registers.

G Major Scales

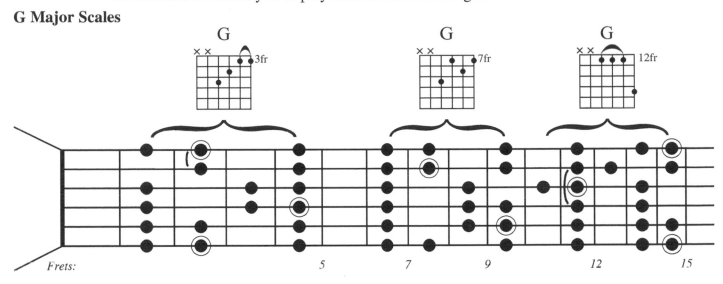

Use the major scales to play melodic solos. The following solo is the melody of the old folk/blues "Careless Love," with a few embellishments (slides and string bends). Check out **ROADMAP #10** for more on string bending. All three moveable G major scale positions are used.

CARELESS LOVE

You can use major scales to improvise. If a song's chord progression doesn't wander too far from the I chord's immediate family, you can often use the major scale of the I chord throughout the tune. In the following I–vi–ii–V progression, the solo makes use of all three G major scale positions.

BOSSA NOVA TUNE

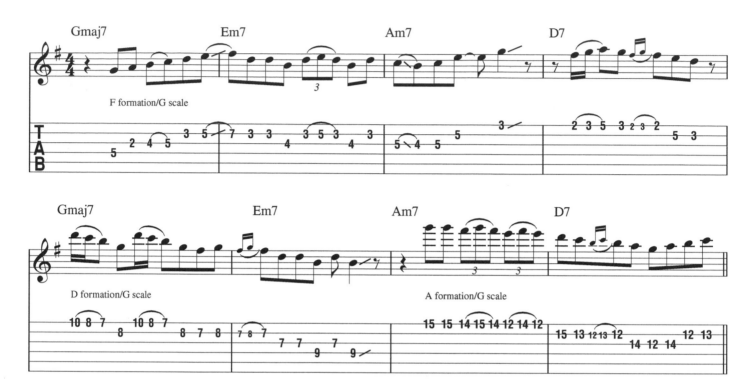

SUMMING UP—NOW YOU KNOW...

1. How to play three moveable major scales for each key.

2. The meaning of the musical term "register."

3. How to play melodies in all keys in two or three registers.

THREE MOVEABLE BLUES SCALES

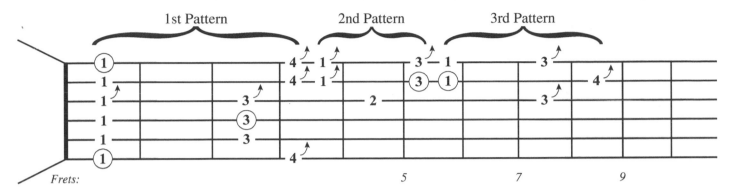

WHY? Blues is the foundation of jazz and rock, and it's a very important element in country, pop, folk, old standards, and show music. Using the blues scales, you can play licks and melodies in all these musical genres. Since the blues scales of **ROADMAP #10** are moveable, they allow you to play in all keys.

WHAT? **The three patterns in ROADMAP #10 are F blues scales.** They are also called *blues boxes* or *minor pentatonic scales*. The root notes are circled. The numbers indicate suggested fingering positions.

The scale notes with arrows (4↗, 1↗) can be bent or "choked." This left-hand technique, described on the next page, is important to the blues sound.

Like the major scales, blues scales are useful for playing melodies as well as licks. Often, you can stay on one blues position and play licks and melodies throughout an entire tune, in spite of chord changes that occur in the tune.

The second and third patterns allow you to play licks and melodies in a higher register than the first pattern. There are still higher patterns, but these three contain the fundamental blues/rock licks and clichés made famous by countless blues, rock, and jazz guitarists.

The blues scale is a *pentatonic* scale, which means it contains five notes: the 1st, ♭3rd, 4th, 5th, and ♭7th notes of your key. For instance, the F minor pentatonic blues scale notes are F, A♭, B♭, C, and E♭—the 1st, ♭3rd, 4th, 5th, and ♭7th notes in relation to the F major scale. The notes of the G blues scale are G(1), B♭(♭3rd), C(4th), D(5th), and F(♭7th).

You can add other notes and still sound bluesy. Here is an expanded version of the three scale patterns with "extra notes" added.

F Blues:

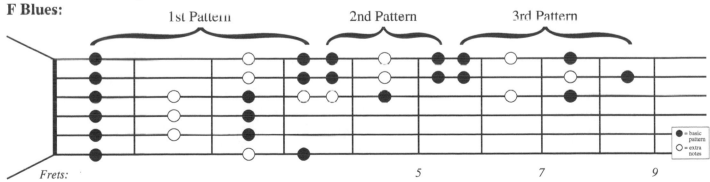

59

HOW?   To put your left hand in position for the first blues box, play an F formation at the appropriate fret. For the key of G, play an F formation at the third fret, which is a G chord. You don't have to maintain the F chord position while playing the scale, but it is a helpful reference point and it contains a high and low root note.

G Blues - First Scale Pattern:

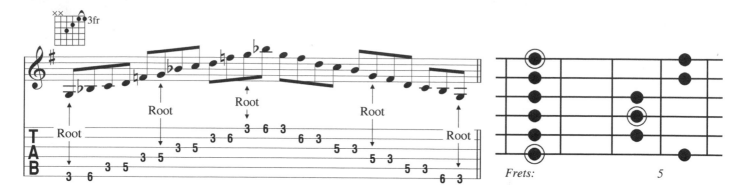

To get your left hand in position for the second blues box, play the root note on the second string with your third (ring) finger. In G, play the G note on the 2nd string/8th fret with your ring finger.

G Blues - Second Scale Pattern:

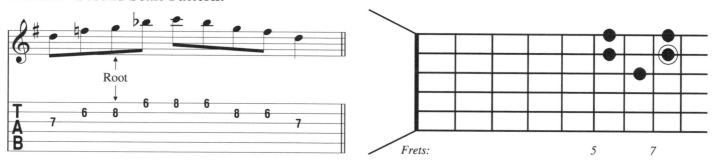

To get your left hand in position for the third blues box, play the F formation of the IV chord. For example, in the key of G, play an F formation/C chord (at the 8th fret), because C is the IV chord in the key of G:

G Blues - Third Scale Pattern:

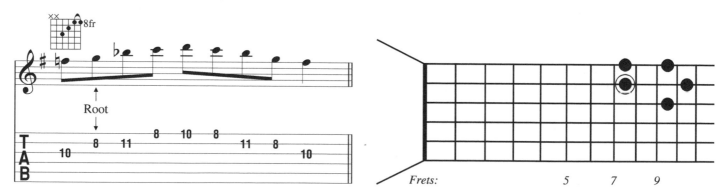

It doesn't sound like blues unless you *choke* (or *bend*) a few strings. To choke a string, you pull it up or down with your fretting finger. This raises its pitch one, two, or three frets higher than usual. You can control the pitch change minutely, and can bend up and down, making a note swoop and glide.

DO IT!

Blues licks: Play these typical blues licks to get the feel of how to use the three scale patterns. Position your left hand appropriately, depending on the blues box you're using.

G Blues - First Scale Pattern

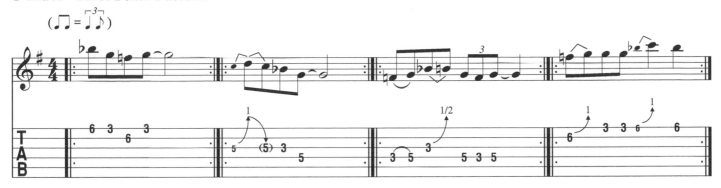

G Blues - Second Scale Pattern

G Blues - Third Scale Pattern

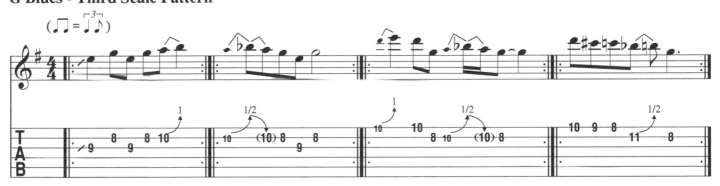

Use the blues boxes to play melodies. Find the melodies to these popular blues and rock tunes, using the first scale pattern: "Pride and Joy," "After Midnight," "Black Magic Woman," Shake, Rattle, and Roll," "Johnny B. Goode," "Evil Ways," "Spoonful," "Route 66," "Hound Dog," "The Thrill Is Gone," "Stormy Monday," and "Baby, Please Don't Go." Bend up to notes that are emphasized to get an extra bluesy effect.

The following version of "See See Rider" is in the key of A. The melody, which is played with some embellishment, resembles "Shake, Rattle, and Roll," and many other popular blues tunes. This arrangement is played in the first blues pattern, except for measures 4–7, which are played in the second pattern. As in many blues tunes, a four-bar phrase is sung twice, followed by a third, rhyming phrase. In this case, the repeated phrase is played an octave higher.

SEE SEE RIDER

See see rid - er, see _____ what you _____ have done. _____

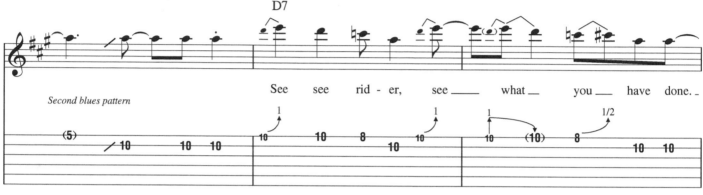

See see rid - er, see _____ what _____ you _____ have done. _____

You made me _____ love you, now _____

_____ your man _____ has come. _____

Play along with recordings (or other players) and ad-lib using the blues scales. You don't have to change patterns with the tune's chord changes. You can play licks in one scale pattern throughout a song.

Relative minor blues scale substitution: If blues licks sound inappropriate in a tune, you can still use the first and second blues boxes: just play them *three frets lower* than the song's actual key. This puts you in the relative minor key. For example, if first-pattern C blues licks (at the 8th fret) don't fit in a key-of-C tune, play first-pattern A blues licks (at the 5th fret) instead. (This works because Am is the relative minor of C, so the *A minor* pentatonic scale is the same as a *C major* pentatonic scale.) This kind of substitution works for many country tunes, rock ballads, or any song whose melody is based on a major scale rather than a blues scale.

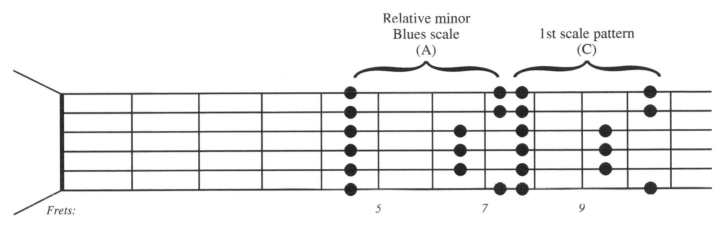

The following version of "Chilly Winds" is in the key of C, and the solo makes use of first and second A blues boxes. Most of the playing is in the first blues pattern, so position your fretting hand in the F formation at the 5th fret. The song is an old blues that has been performed by many country, folk, bluegrass, and rock artists.

CHILLY WINDS

You can use the third blues box to play non-blues tunes. Like the "substitute scale" described above, the third blues pattern works in situations where the first two blues patterns sound inappropriate. The country-rock tune below illustrates this:

THE WATER IS WIDE

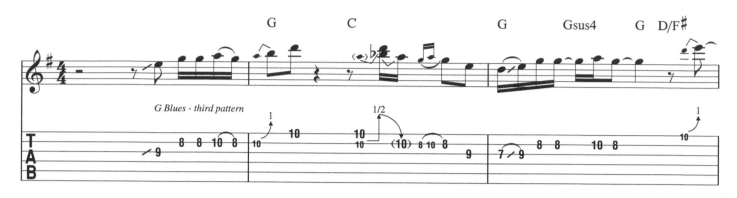

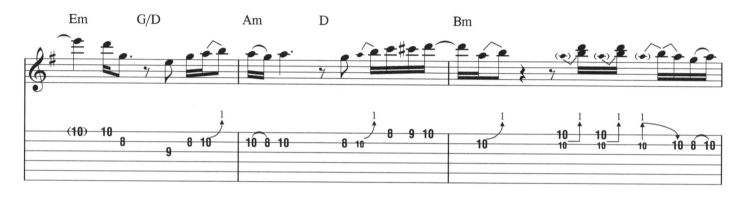

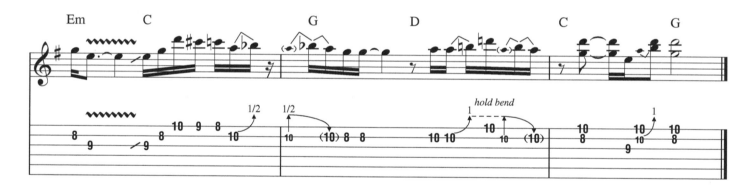

SUMMING UP—NOW YOU KNOW...

1. How to play blues licks and melodies in any key, using three different scale patterns (blues boxes).

2. How to choke (bend) strings for a bluesy effect.

3. The notes that make up the pentatonic blues scale.

4. How to substitute the relative minor blues scale when the standard blues licks don't fit in a tune.

MAJOR PENTATONIC SCALES

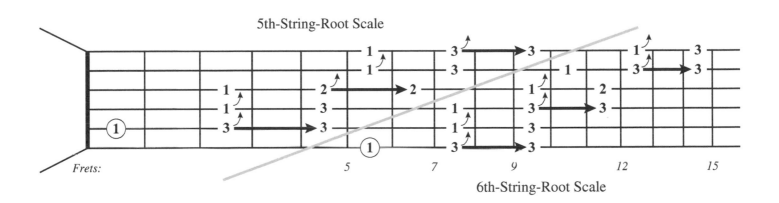

5th-String-Root Scale

Frets:

6th-String-Root Scale

WHY? These two versatile scales can help you solo and play backup licks in rock, R&B, country, jazz, blues, bluegrass, folk, and pop tunes.

WHAT? **ROADMAP #11 illustrates how to play two B♭ major pentatonic scales.** One has a 6th-string root, the other a 5th-string root. (Both roots are circled.)

These scales include "built-in" slides, indicated by straight arrows. As a result, each scale spans ten frets.

Numbers on the fretboard with curved arrows (3 ↗, 1 ↗) can be bent (choked).

Often, one sliding scale can be played throughout a tune. If a tune is in the key of C, you can use C sliding scales throughout.

— **You can also "go with the changes"** and use the sliding scale that matches each chord change, especially when a song stays on a chord for more than a few bars.

The major pentatonic scale contains these five notes: 1, 2, 3, 5, and 6. In the key of C, that's: C(1), D(2), E(3), G(5), and A(6). Just hum the "My Girl" riff to remember the major pentatonic sound.

Use the major pentatonic scales to play licks and melodies in all kinds of music, whenever blues scales sound inappropriate. You can hear classic major-pentatonic "noodling" in the solos of Dicky Betts (Allman Brothers) and Jerry Garcia (Grateful Dead). For classic rock examples, listen to the Allman Brothers' "Ramblin' Man," George Harrison's solo in the Beatles' "Let It Be," and Ron Wood's lead guitar in Rod Stewart's "Maggie May."

HOW? Play both scales over and over to become familiar with them.

C Major Pentatonic Scale (5th String Root)

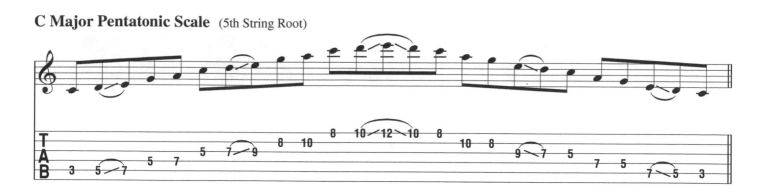

C Major Pentatonic Scale (6th String Root)

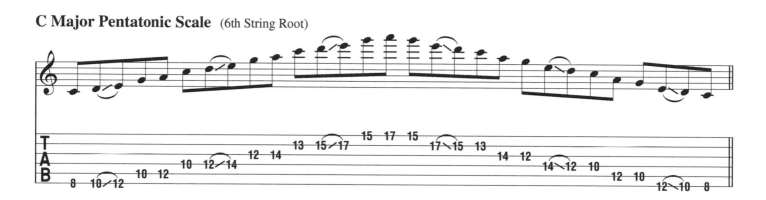

DO IT! The next three solos are composed of C and G major pentatonic licks:

Fast Country Rock

Slow Rock

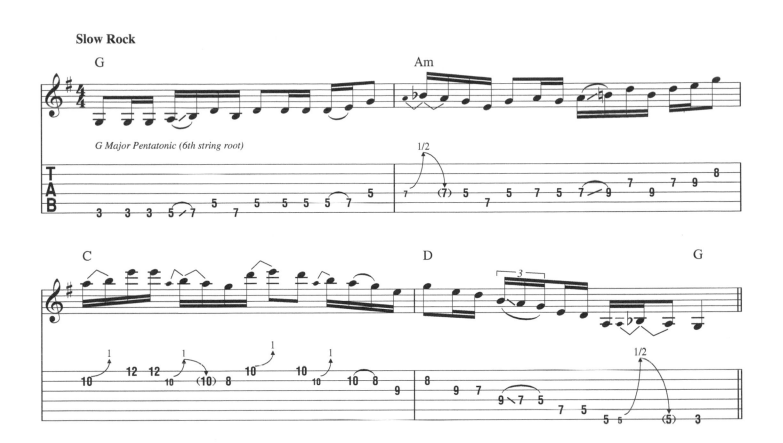

G Major Pentatonic (6th string root)

Country Shuffle (♪♪ = ♪ ♪³)

C (5th string root)

Play along with recordings or other players, and use the major pentatonic scales as guidelines for your improvising. Try staying in the tonic (key center) scale position throughout a song, and then try using a different scale to match each chord change.

Play this version of "Chilly Winds" in the key of G. The melody is played with some embellishment, using the 6th-string-root G major pentatonic scale. The second eight measures are up an octave from the first eight measures.

CHILLY WINDS (G Pentatonic Scale)

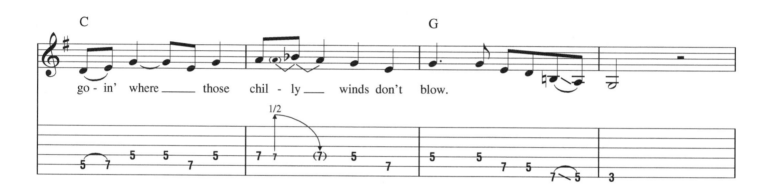

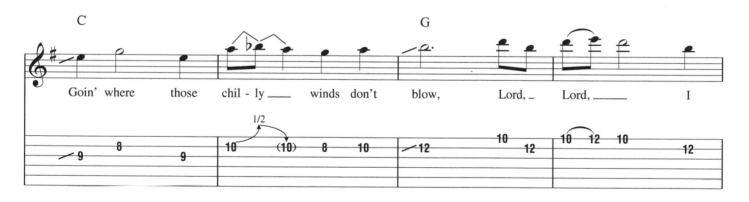

The following solo goes "with the changes." It has the same chord progression as the previous "Chilly Winds," but the solo is based on the G major pentatonic scale during the G chord, the C major pentatonic scale during the C chord, and the D scale during the D chord.

CHILLY WINDS (going "with the changes")

SUMMING UP—NOW YOU KNOW...

1. Two major pentatonic scales for each key and how to use them for soloing.

2. How to solo "with the changes" using major pentatonic scales.

A MOVEABLE DOUBLE-NOTE LICK

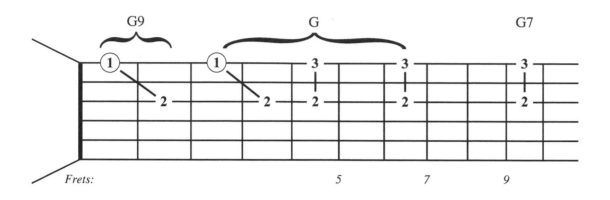

WHY? This moveable double-note pattern opens up a whole "bag of licks" for lead guitar. It's the basis for many licks and solos, in all musical genres, and it's the source of many classic rock and R&B riffs (listen to Van Morrison's "Brown Eyed Girl," Jimi Hendrix's "Red House" intro, and Sam & Dave's "Soul Man").

WHAT? **It's basically a key-of-E blues turnaround** *made into a moveable lick.* Here's the original turnaround, followed by a moveable version:

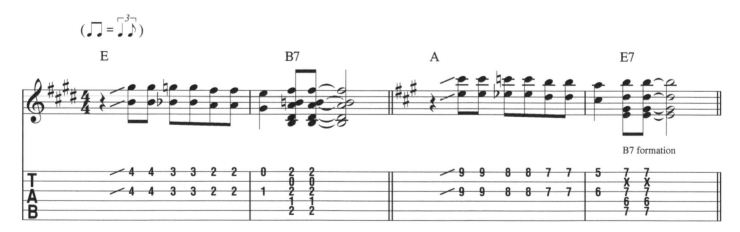

"Home base" for this series of licks is the F formation. To play the above turnaround in G, position your fretting hand at the third-fret F formation. Begin the lick by sliding up to the 7th fret, using the fingering indicated in **ROADMAP #12**.

70

There are countless double-note licks that spring from this roadmap. They can be played as backup fills, during solos, and as "riffs" (repetitious signature licks that give a tune a distinct character). They can go up, down, or up and down, as shown by these variations on a G chord:

The G9 and G7 shown in **ROADMAP #12** offer still more variations. (See examples in the **DO IT!** section.)

HOW?

Change F formations with the tune's chord changes: When there is a C chord, play double-note licks based on the F-formation C chord at the 8th fret.

You can start a lick at any of the five positions of ROADMAP #12—not just at the F formation. The F formation is for orientation. You can visualize the F formation/home base and play the positions that are above or below it, as in the second example above (starting at the top and coming down). There are more examples in the **DO IT!** section.

"In-between" positions can be used. For example, the original turnaround in G includes a double-note on the 6th fret, between the standard 5th- and 7th-fret double-notes.

DO IT!

Play the following double-note licks. They illustrate a few of the many musical styles you can enhance with this bag of tricks.

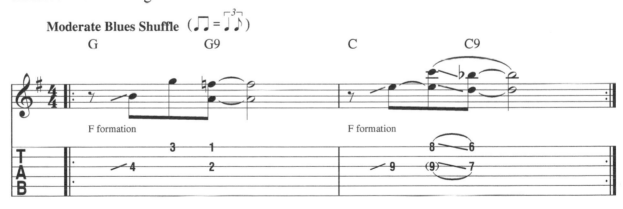

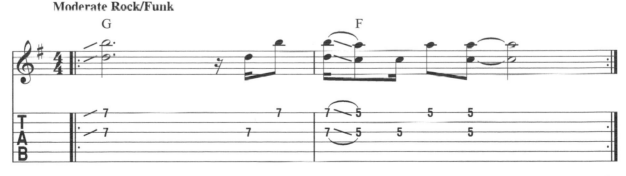

Moderate Rock/Funk

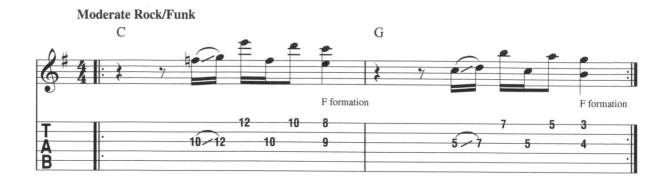

Moderate Rock, from D(V) to G(I)

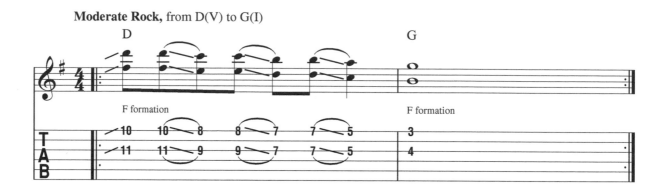

Moderate Country Waltz

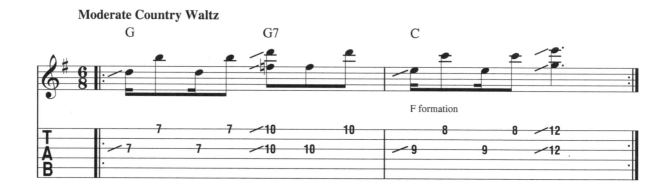

Moderate Country Shuffle

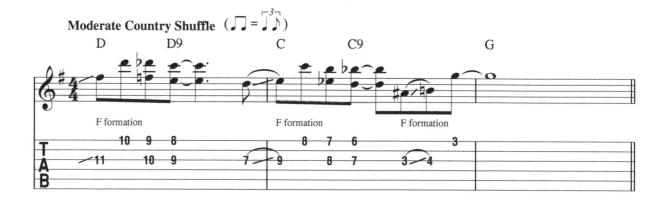

— Notice how conveniently the tonic 7th position leads to the IV chord in the "country waltz" lick. The 7th chord usually leads "up a fourth." So, play the G7 position before going to C, or the C7 double-note lick to lead to an F, etc.

— The 9th position has a bluesy flavor.

If your guitar has a cutaway, you can often choose a higher or lower position for any chord. For example, you can base the G licks on the F formation/3rd fret or the F formation/15th fret.

The following rock version of the old blues "Stagolee" shows how to use the double-note licks as fills, during a vocal, and in solos. Notice how the tonic 7th position (G7, measure 4 of the solo) leads to the IV chord (C). The 9th position also leads "up a fourth," as illustrated in measures 9–10 of the solo: The D9 position leads to G.

STAGOLEE

"Careless Love," below, is another example of how to use the double-note licks as fills behind a vocalist, and how to use them to build a solo.

CARELESS LOVE

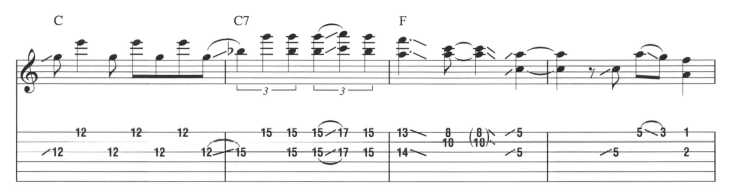

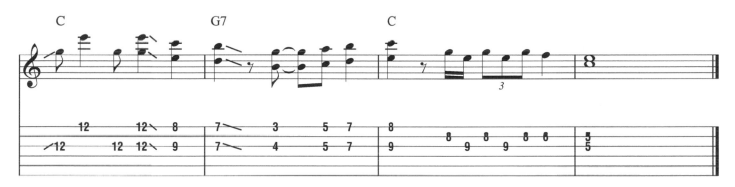

SUMMING UP—NOW YOU KNOW...

1. How to play a series of double-note licks on the first and third strings for solos or backup, in any key.

2. That 7th or 9th chords often lead "up a fourth."

WHAT NEXT?

If you have read all twelve roadmaps/chapters and played all the licks and exercises, you may be wondering where to go from here. A few suggestions:

- If a roadmap opens up uncharted territory for you, it may take days or weeks of playing to assimilate the information. Think about the new material whenever you play, and try to use it.

- The roadmaps are especially helpful for playing with other people—jamming, improvising. Find some other players, and play along with recordings, too.

- Listen to recordings (and the radio) and try to recognize scales and licks from the roadmaps. Try to imitate what you hear.

- **Improvise!** The roadmaps will take you to new places on the guitar.

There are genre-specific roadmaps books/CDs, to enhance your understanding of various musical styles:
— *Fretboard Roadmaps for Blues Guitar*
— *Fretboard Roadmaps for Jazz Guitar*
— *Fretboard Roadmaps for Rock Guitar*
— *Fretboard Roadmaps for Country Guitar*
— *Fretboard Roadmaps for Bluegrass/Folk Guitar*
— *Fretboard Roadmaps for Slide Guitar*
— *Fretboard Roadmaps for Dobro Guitar*
— *Fretboard Roadmaps for 5-String Banjo*
— *Fretboard Roadmaps for Mandolin*
— *Fretboard Roadmaps for Bass Guitar*
— *Fretboard Roadmaps for Ukulele*

Direct questions you may have about this book or other Fred Sokolow books to *Sokolowmusic.com*.

Happy navigating/picking!

Fred Sokolow

ABOUT THE AUTHOR

FRED SOKOLOW is a versatile "musician's musician." Besides fronting his own jazz, bluegrass, and rock bands, Fred has toured with Bobbie Gentry, Jim Stafford, Tom Paxton, Ian Whitcomb, Jody Stecher and The Limeliters, playing guitar, banjo, mandolin, and Dobro. His music has been heard on many TV shows (*Survivor, Dr. Quinn*), commercials, and movies (listen for his Dixieland-style banjo in *The Cat's Meow*).

Sokolow has written nearly a hundred stringed instrument books and videos for seven major publishers. This library of instructional material, which teaches jazz, rock, bluegrass, country, and blues guitar, banjo, Dobro, and mandolin, is sold on six continents. He also teaches musical seminars on the West Coast. A jazz CD, two rock guitar and two banjo recordings, which showcase Sokolow's technique, all received excellent reviews in the U.S. and Europe.

If you think Sokolow still isn't versatile enough, know that he emceed for Carol Doda at San Francisco's legendary Condor Club, accompanied a Russian balalaika virtuoso at the swank Bonaventure Hotel in L.A., won the *Gong Show*, played lap steel and banjo on the *Tonight Show*, picked Dobro with Chubby Checker, and played mandolin with Rick James.

GUITAR NOTATION LEGEND

Guitar music can be notated three different ways: on a *musical staff*, in *tablature*, and in *rhythm slashes*.

RHYTHM SLASHES are written above the staff. Strum chords in the rhythm indicated. Use the chord diagrams found at the top of the first page of the transcription for the appropriate chord voicings. Round noteheads indicate single notes.

THE MUSICAL STAFF shows pitches and rhythms and is divided by bar lines into measures. Pitches are named after the first seven letters of the alphabet.

TABLATURE graphically represents the guitar fingerboard. Each horizontal line represents a string, and each number represents a fret.

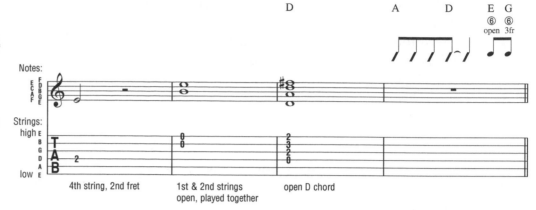

4th string, 2nd fret   1st & 2nd strings open, played together   open D chord

DEFINITIONS FOR SPECIAL GUITAR NOTATION

HALF-STEP BEND: Strike the note and bend up 1/2 step.

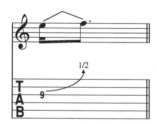

WHOLE-STEP BEND: Strike the note and bend up one step.

GRACE NOTE BEND: Strike the note and immediately bend up as indicated.

SLIGHT (MICROTONE) BEND: Strike the note and bend up 1/4 step.

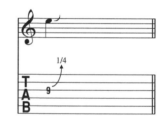

BEND AND RELEASE: Strike the note and bend up as indicated, then release back to the original note. Only the first note is struck.

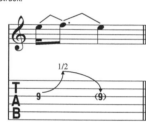

PRE-BEND: Bend the note as indicated, then strike it.

PRE-BEND AND RELEASE: Bend the note as indicated. Strike it and release the bend back to the original note.

UNISON BEND: Strike the two notes simultaneously and bend the lower note up to the pitch of the higher.

VIBRATO: The string is vibrated by rapidly bending and releasing the note with the fretting hand.

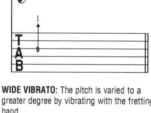

WIDE VIBRATO: The pitch is varied to a greater degree by vibrating with the fretting hand.

HAMMER-ON: Strike the first (lower) note with one finger, then sound the higher note (on the same string) with another finger by fretting it without picking.

PULL-OFF: Place both fingers on the notes to be sounded. Strike the first note and without picking, pull the finger off to sound the second (lower) note.

LEGATO SLIDE: Strike the first note and then slide the same fret-hand finger up or down to the second note. The second note is not struck.

SHIFT SLIDE: Same as legato slide, except the second note is struck.

TRILL: Very rapidly alternate between the notes indicated by continuously hammering on and pulling off.

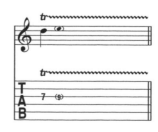

TAPPING: Hammer ("tap") the fret indicated with the pick-hand index or middle finger and pull off to the note fretted by the fret hand.

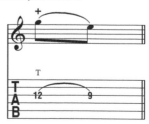

NATURAL HARMONIC: Strike the note while the fret-hand lightly touches the string directly over the fret indicated.

PINCH HARMONIC: The note is fretted normally and a harmonic is produced by adding the edge of the thumb or the tip of the index finger of the pick hand to the normal pick attack.

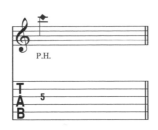

HARP HARMONIC: The note is fretted normally and a harmonic is produced by gently resting the pick hand's index finger directly above the indicated fret (in parentheses) while the pick hand's thumb or pick assists by plucking the appropriate string.

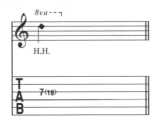

PICK SCRAPE: The edge of the pick is rubbed down (or up) the string, producing a scratchy sound.

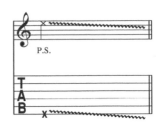

MUFFLED STRINGS: A percussive sound is produced by laying the fret hand across the string(s) without depressing, and striking them with the pick hand.

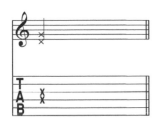

PALM MUTING: The note is partially muted by the pick hand lightly touching the string(s) just before the bridge.

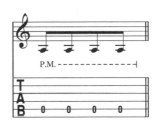

RAKE: Drag the pick across the strings indicated with a single motion.

TREMOLO PICKING: The note is picked as rapidly and continuously as possible.

ARPEGGIATE: Play the notes of the chord indicated by quickly rolling them from bottom to top.

VIBRATO BAR DIVE AND RETURN: The pitch of the note or chord is dropped a specified number of steps (in rhythm), then returned to the original pitch.

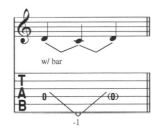

VIBRATO BAR SCOOP: Depress the bar just before striking the note, then quickly release the bar.

VIBRATO BAR DIP: Strike the note and then immediately drop a specified number of steps, then release back to the original pitch.

ADDITIONAL MUSICAL DEFINITIONS

(accent)	• Accentuate note (play it louder).	
(accent)	• Accentuate note with great intensity.	
(staccato)	• Play the note short.	
◻	• Downstroke	
V	• Upstroke	

D.S. al Coda • Go back to the sign (𝄋), then play until the measure marked "*To Coda*," then skip to the section labelled "*Coda*."

D.C. al Fine • Go back to the beginning of the song and play until the measure marked "*Fine*" (end).

Rhy. Fig. • Label used to recall a recurring accompaniment pattern (usually chordal).

Riff • Label used to recall composed, melodic lines (usually single notes) which recur.

Fill • Label used to identify a brief melodic figure which is to be inserted into the arrangement.

Rhy. Fill • A chordal version of a Fill.

tacet • Instrument is silent (drops out).

• Repeat measures between signs.

• When a repeated section has different endings, play the first ending only the first time and the second ending only the second time.

NOTE: Tablature numbers in parentheses mean:
1. The note is being sustained over a system (note in standard notation is tied), or
2. The note is sustained, but a new articulation (such as a hammer-on, pull-off, slide or vibrato) begins, or
3. The note is a barely audible "ghost" note (note in standard notation is also in parentheses).

Get Better at Guitar

...with these Great Guitar Instruction Books from Hal Leonard!

101 GUITAR TIPS
STUFF ALL THE PROS KNOW AND USE
by Adam St. James
This book contains invaluable guidance on everything from scales and music theory to truss rod adjustments, proper recording studio set-ups, and much more.
00695737 Book/Online Audio $17.99

AMAZING PHRASING
by Tom Kolb
This book/audio pack explores all the main components necessary for crafting well-balanced rhythmic and melodic phrases. It also explains how these phrases are put together to form cohesive solos. The companion audio contains 89 demo tracks, most with full-band backing.
00695583 Book/Online Audio $22.99

ARPEGGIOS FOR THE MODERN GUITARIST
by Tom Kolb
Using this no-nonsense book with online audio, guitarists will learn to apply and execute all types of arpeggio forms using a variety of techniques, including alternate picking, sweep picking, tapping, string skipping, and legato.
00695862 Book/Online Audio $22.99

BLUES YOU CAN USE
by John Ganapes
This comprehensive source for learning blues guitar is designed to develop both your lead and rhythm playing. Includes: 21 complete solos • blues chords, progressions and riffs • turnarounds • movable scales and soloing techniques • string bending • utilizing the entire fingerboard • and more.
00142420 Book/Online Media.................................$22.99

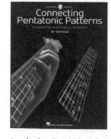

CONNECTING PENTATONIC PATTERNS
by Tom Kolb
If you've been finding yourself trapped in the pentatonic box, this book is for you! This hands-on book with online audio offers examples for guitar players of all levels, from beginner to advanced. Study this book faithfully, and soon you'll be soloing all over the neck with the greatest of ease.
00696445 Book/Online Audio $24.99

FRETBOARD MASTERY
by Troy Stetina
Untangle the mysterious regions of the guitar fretboard and unlock your potential. This book familiarizes you with all the shapes you need to know by applying them in real musical examples, thereby reinforcing and reaffirming your newfound knowledge.
00695331 Book/Online Audio $22.99

GUITAR AEROBICS
by Troy Nelson
Here is a daily dose of guitar "vitamins" to keep your chops fine tuned! Musical styles include rock, blues, jazz, metal, country, and funk. Techniques taught include alternate picking, arpeggios, sweep picking, string skipping, legato, string bending, and rhythm guitar.
00695946 Book/Online Audio $24.99

GUITAR CLUES
OPERATION PENTATONIC
by Greg Koch
Whether you're new to improvising or have been doing it for a while, this book/audio pack will provide loads of delicious licks and tricks that you can use right away, from volume swells and chicken pickin' to intervallic and chordal ideas.
00695827 Book/Online Audio $24.99

PAT METHENY – GUITAR ETUDES
Over the years, in many master classes and workshops around the world, Pat has demonstrated the kind of daily workout he puts himself through. This book includes a collection of 14 guitar etudes he created to help you limber up, improve picking technique and build finger independence.
00696587...$17.99

PICTURE CHORD ENCYCLOPEDIA
This comprehensive guitar chord resource for all playing styles and levels features five voicings of 44 chord qualities for all twelve keys – 2,640 chords in all! For each, there is a clearly illustrated chord frame, as well as *an actual photo* of the chord being played!.
00695224...$22.99

RHYTHM GUITAR 365
by Troy Nelson
This book provides 365 exercises – one for every day of the year! – to keep your rhythm chops fine tuned. Topics covered include: chord theory; the fundamentals of rhythm; fingerpicking; strum patterns; diatonic and non-diatonic progressions; triads; major and minor keys; and more.
00103627 Book/Online Audio $27.99

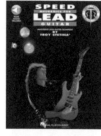

SCALE CHORD RELATIONSHIPS
by Michael Mueller & Jeff Schroedl
This book/audio pack explains how to: recognize keys • analyze chord progressions • use the modes • play over nondiatonic harmony • use harmonic and melodic minor scales • use symmetrical scales • incorporate exotic scales • and much more!
00695563 Book/Online Audio $17.99

SPEED MECHANICS FOR LEAD GUITAR
by Troy Stetina
Take your playing to the stratosphere with this advanced lead book which will help you develop speed and precision in today's explosive playing styles. Learn the fastest ways to achieve speed and control, secrets to make your practice time really count, and how to open your ears and make your musical ideas more solid and tangible.
00699323 Book/Online Audio $22.99

TOTAL ROCK GUITAR
by Troy Stetina
This comprehensive source for learning rock guitar is designed to develop both your lead and rhythm playing. It covers: getting a tone that rocks • open chords, power chords and barre chords • riffs, scales and licks • string bending, strumming, and harmonics • and more.
00695246 Book/Online Audio $22.99

Guitar World Presents
STEVE VAI'S GUITAR WORKOUT
In this book, Steve Vai reveals his path to virtuoso enlightenment with two challenging guitar workouts – one 10-hour and one 30-hour – which include scale and chord exercises, ear training, sight-reading, music theory, and much more.
00119643...$16.99

HAL•LEONARD®